The Wharf Street Vegetarian Café Cookbook

A unique collection of international recipes and original ideas from a small, independent and very special restaurant, interwoven with fascinating glimpses of café life in words and pictures.

The Wharf Street Vegetarian Café Cookbook

Jill Gibbon

with illustrations by the author

THORSONS PUBLISHING GROUP

*Wellingborough * New York*

First published 1986

© JILL GIBBON 1986

Gibbon, Jill
The Wharf Street vegetarian café cookbook.
1. Cookery (vegetarian)
I. Title
641.6'5   TX801

ISBN 0 7225 1224 4

Printed and bound in Great Britain

'He's had some sort of dashed fit,' I said. I took another look. 'Jeeves! Someone's been feeding him meat!'

— *Carry on Jeeves*: P.G. Wodehouse

ACKNOWLEDGEMENTS

Many thanks to everyone who has helped me with this book, giving recipes, testing and tasting them and making suggestions . . . but especially Stacey for all her encouragement and enthusiasm, my father for hours of typing, criticism and proofreading, and Tom for comments on the pictures. And best wishes to all who have ever worked or eaten at the Café.

CONTENTS

INTRODUCTION

The Wharf Street Café is a wholefood, vegetarian restaurant in the back streets of Leeds. It is a small Victorian building with wide, high windows, an arch in the middle and bricked yard at the back where stables used to be. Herbs and flowers grow there now, and in the summer customers sit out at tables or up on the stable steps. In other seasons they crowd into the often too small dining rooms. The kitchen is also very small, and the cooks have to learn to dance round each other from the chopping boards to the cookers and sink and back again. Nevertheless, great feats of cooking are performed — pies, pizzas, bread, salads, soups and bakes are made for lunchtime and exotic menus for evening International Nights.

The History of the Café

The Café is a workers' co-op — a business owned and controlled by its workers. The Co-operative Movement dates from the early nineteenth century but experienced a wave of new interest in the 1970s, no doubt in response to rising unemployment on the one hand, and job dissatisfaction on the other. At this time co-ops of all kinds sprang up in Leeds: in car repair, shoe-making, printing, building, laundry — and a cluster in wholefoods. A wholefood warehousing co-op called Suma set up on Wharf Street to distribute wholefoods to shops in the north of England. Beano, the wholefood shop, followed in a neighbouring street, thus providing Suma with a Leeds outlet, after which a bagging co-op formed within Suma to pack their pre-packed goods. A little later, the Wharf Street Café was started in a disused café, giving the workers in these new co-ops somewhere to lunch and Leeds its first wholefood restaurant. Despite such linked beginnings these co-ops were always separate businesses, although with strong bonds of friendship and trade. The clustering around a few local streets has inevitably changed as the co-ops have grown. Beano has moved to a larger shop in central Leeds and Suma has plans to move to a new warehouse in Halifax. It is sad to lose the original closeness, but it is most encouraging to see that co-ops are beginning to prosper.

Co-operative working has its own rewards and difficulties. Co-ops are often set up with very little money and equipment, so the work can be long and arduous and the wages low. But everyone is equally responsible for the running of the business and that is very fulfilling.

Who does What?

At the Café everyone takes a share in all the necessary jobs — the menu-planning, food buying, book-keeping, redecorating, cooking, serving and washing up. Problems and future plans are discussed at weekly meetings, upstairs from a circle of armchairs. There is always a sense at these times that if only this was reorganized, or that changed, or the right-hand kitchen wall moved a bit more to the right, everything would be easier — and so we go on talking late into the night.

Although never dull, the life is extremely exhausting; consequently many, many cooks have passed through over the years. Every one, however, has brought new ideas and recipes: new cakes — an orange and poppy-seed cake or a fruit and cream gateau; vegetable and grain bakes or finely chopped jewel-coloured salads; creamy soups or a spicy dahl. The recipes, variations, tips and ideas are passed on from cook to cook and become a part of the Café. And it is something of the fruits of this tradition that we hope to pass on to you in this book.

A couple of notes before the recipes

Quantities are given in Imperial and Metric measurements — please follow one or the other but not a mixture of both. All of the recipes are intended for six people unless otherwise stated.

BREADS

Home baked bread with the mealy flavour of ripe
wheat roundly in your mouth.
— *How Green Was My Valley*: Richard Llewellyn.

A large bowl of bread dough is mixed each morning at the Café as soon as the first worker arrives. It rises while everyone has a breakfast of toasted bread left over from the day before, scrambled or poached eggs, jam, peanut butter, tea (chosen from a wide variety of types) and sleepy conversation around a table in the dining room. Everyone slowly wakes up and the lunchtime menu is planned and shared out. Then the day's cooking gets underway and the dough is kneaded into rolls and loaves and left to rise for a second time over the stoves now hot with pots of soup and vegetables. And by noon Wharf Street is full of the smells of lunch, and in particular the smell of baking bread.

The Secrets of Successful Bread

Breadmaking has a few essential rules but so long as these are followed it is foolproof and satisfying and can soon become part of the daily or weekly routine of any kitchen. The rising stage is crucial and depends on the yeast and the temperature. Always use warm water, warm hands, and a warm bowl and find a warm place for the dough to rise in.

Temperature   In winter, winds sweep up and down the archway that runs through the centre of the Café, and the kitchen is icy until cooking has started. The cooks arrive swathed in thick coats and scarves, comparing the number of jumpers and vests they have been compelled to put on — but these are progressively shed during the course of the morning. At such times the flour and bowl are warmed in a low oven to take the chill off before starting, and the bread dough is put on a chair in front of the dining room heater for its first rise. In the summer, sunlight streams into the dining room, so the dough is simply left on a table in the window.

Yeast   There are three main types of yeast for breadmaking, fresh yeast, instant dried yeast and dried yeast. Fresh yeast has

a life of only two weeks in the fridge and must be 'started' (i.e., mixed with a sweetener to start the rising process before it is added to the flour.) It is slower and less convenient than the other yeasts but it gives the bread a fuller, yeasted flavour and it is enjoyable to watch it froth and rise. Sometimes a little fresh yeast is bought on a whim with the Café's weekly shopping and used in a batch of bread, so there is a fresh yeast bread recipe towards the end of this chapter. However we usually use instant dried yeast as it is quick and reliable, and this is the yeast referred to in the other bread recipes. There is no need to start it, so it can be mixed straight in with the other ingredients. It can be kept for up to six months in an airtight container but after this it becomes rather inefficient. Dried yeast must be started in the same way as fresh yeast but it has a similar life span to instant dried yeast. In my experience it tends to be undependable, so I wouldn't recommend it.

Oil   The chief function of oil in bread is to add moisture. If you are feeling extravagant, olive oil or coldpressed corn oil also bring flavour, and to make the most of this you can use quite a bit more than is indicated in the basic recipe. Otherwise, soya oil is good and cheap and this is the oil that we usually use for breadmaking in the Café.

Milk   Milk can be used in breadmaking but should always be scalded first (i.e., heated to just below boiling point) to destroy the enzymes that can inhibit yeast action. Milk makes a slightly cakier bread and so is particularly suitable in the sweeter, honey loaves.

Flour   Flours vary a great deal and make a vast difference to the taste, texture and weight of your bread. The Café uses soft wheat or English wheat for all its baking. It is a crumbly flour making a 'caky' bread-chewy, moist and tasty, and can be bought stone-ground and organically grown from most

13

wholefood shops. Hard wheat or American wheat has a much higher gluten content than the English wheat and so is more elastic. It is available stone-ground from supermarkets, often sold as 'Bread Flour' and sometimes called 'Strong Flour'. Use this if you want to make a lighter, more shop-like bread.

Different types of flour soak up differing amounts of water so you may find you need more or less flour than the quantity given in the recipe. Just use enough to bring the dough to the right consistency.

WHARF STREET BREAD

**1 teaspoon honey and/
or malt and/
or molasses
1 heaped teaspoon sea salt
1 pint (570ml) hand-hot water
1 tablespoon oil
1½ tablespoons instant dried yeast
2 lb (900g) wholewheat flour (approx.)
Poppyseeds or sesame seeds**

Dissolve the honey, malt, molasses and salt in the water in a large bowl. Then stir in the oil, dried yeast and ¾ of the flour to make a sticky, wet batter. Leave to rise in a warm place for 30 minutes until it has doubled in size.

Add the rest of the flour and stir it into a stiff dough. Tip out onto a well-floured board, cover your hands with flour and knead. Fold the dough in half towards you, pummel it, turn it and fold it in half towards you again. Repeat over and over, adding more flour as necessary until it is elastic, firm and still slightly moist. Divide into two and knead each piece into an oval shape. They should be large enough to half-fill two large bread tins.

Oil each tin well and scatter poppyseeds or sesame seeds over the bottom. Push in the dough, pummel down, then tip it out again and replace the other way up. This gives the loaf a good shape and coats it with oil and seeds. Score the top two or three times with a knife; then leave to rise again for 20-30 minutes until the dough has reached the top of the tins.

Meanwhile pre-heat the oven to Gas Mark 6 (400°F/200°C). Bake 40-50 minutes. Baking times differ with flour types and ovens, but after a while as you get to know the flour you use, and your oven, you will get a more exact baking time for your own bread. To test, tip the loaves out of their tins and tap their bases — if they sound hollow, they are done. The loaves can be left to bake out of their tins for 5 minutes or so to give a crisp crust. When they are out of the oven, leave to cool on a wire cake rack, or upside down, bases upwards. This allows the air to circulate freely around the loaves, cooling them evenly.

KNEADING · KNEADING · KNEADING · KNEADING · KNEADING · KNEADING · KNEADING · KNEADING · KNEADING · K

Variations All sorts of things can be added to a bread dough, spare cooked grains, dried fruit, herbs, depending on what's in your kitchen and what takes your fancy. As in the basic recipe, the quantities in each variation are for two loaves. If you like, you can make just one varied and one plain loaf, by dividing the basic dough into two bowls and adding just half the quantities given for the variation into one. And in this way you can also make two different kinds of varied loaves at a time — a fruit loaf and a herb loaf, or a honey loaf and a garlic loaf, giving a choice of sweet or savoury . . .

OAT BREAD

**3 oz (75g) rolled oats
½ pint (285ml) water
½ pint (285ml) milk
1 dessertspoon honey**

Soak the oats in the water for at least an hour (or overnight). Scald the milk (i.e., heat until it is just about to boil), stir in the honey, cool a little and mix with the oats and water. Make a bread batter as in the basic recipe, using 3 oz (75g) less flour.

ONION BREAD

1 onion
1 tablespoon butter (or olive oil)
1 teaspoon celery seeds

Dice the onion very fine and sauté in the butter with the celery seeds until soft and just turning golden. Cool a little and add to the bread dough after the first rise.

YOGURT AND CARAWAY SEED BREAD

1 dessertspoon malt
1 teaspoon honey
¼ pint (150ml) yogurt
1 tablespoon caraway seeds

Make a bread batter using only ¾ pint (425ml) warm water and the malt and honey as the sweetener. Mix in the yogurt and caraway seeds and proceed as usual.

WHEAT BREAD

3 oz (75g) wheat berries
1 tablespoon honey
1 tablespoon poppyseeds
2 tablespoons sesame seeds

Bring the wheat berries to the boil in plenty of water and simmer for two hours adding more water as necessary. The wheat should be very soft and beginning to break open.

Start the bread during the wheat's second hour of cooking and set to rise in the warmth of the pan. Use the honey as the sweetener in the batter.

When cooked rinse the wheat in a little water to cool and add to the dough with the seeds after the first rise.

GARLIC AND THYME BREAD

¼ pint (150ml) boiling water
2 tablespoons thyme
4-6 cloves garlic

Pour the boiling water over the thyme and leave to soak for an hour. Dice the garlic very fine. Add both to a bread batter made as usual but with only ¾ pint (425ml) warm water.

HERB BREAD

¼ pint (150ml) boiling water
1 tablespoon marjoram
1 tablespoon basil
1 tablespoon oregano

Pour the boiling water over the chopped fresh herbs and leave to soak for an hour.

Add to the bread batter made as usual but with only ¾ pint (425ml) warm water.

KIBBLED WHEAT LOAF

Kibbled wheat is whole wheat grain, cracked on a millstone. It can be mixed into the bread dough without pre-cooking, and adds chewiness and taste.

1 tablespoon malt
1 tablespoon honey
4 oz (110g) kibbled wheat
1 tablespoon poppy seeds and extra for scattering
over the tops

Make a bread batter as usual, using the malt and honey as the sweetener and adding the kibbled wheat and poppy seeds with the first of the flour. Scatter a few poppy seeds over the tops when shaping the loaves.

□   □   □   □   □   □   □   □   □

HONEY AND WHEATGERM BREAD

½ pint (285ml) warm milk
2-3 tablespoons honey (and a little extra for glazing)
4 oz (110g) wheat germ

Scald the milk (i.e., heat until it is just about to boil). Stir in the honey and cool a little. Pour in a large bowl, stir in the wheatgerm and make a bread batter as in the basic recipe, using 4 oz (110g) less flour, and only ½ pint (285ml) warm water. When the loaves are out of the oven, paint the tops with a wet brush dipped in honey.

□   □   □   □   □   □   □   □   □

FRUIT BREAD

1 dessertspoon malt
1 dessertspoon honey (and a little extra for glazing)
4 oz (110g) sultanas
4 oz (110g) currants
1 teaspoon cinnamon
¼ teaspoon nutmeg

Make a bread batter using the malt and honey as the sweetener. Mix in the dried fruit and spices and proceed as usual.

When the loaves are out of the oven paint the tops with a wet brush dipped in the honey.

SESAME SEED ROLLS

For many years the wholefood shop Beano was just around the corner from the Café. Every morning a basketful of warm, steaming rolls would be hurried over there as soon as the first batch came out of the ovens. And the shop workers, waiting for their breakfasts, would take four or five rolls to the back of the shop to eat while the rest were put up onto a shelf to be sold.

Soft inside, with a crisp crust of sesame seeds on top, these are best eaten fresh the same day. Makes 12-16 rolls.

1 egg, beaten in a shallow bowl
Sesame seeds generously poured into a second
shallow bowl

Make a bread dough as usual. After kneading, divide the dough into balls, each weighing roughly 3-4 oz (75-100g). Dip the top of each roll into the beaten egg and then into the seeds. Arrange on a well-oiled tray with a little space around each and leave in a warm place for 15-20 minutes to rise.

Meanwhile, preheat the oven to Gas Mark 7 (425°F/220°C). Bake for 20-25 minutes.

SULTANA BUNS

Makes about 8 buns. Eaten warm and spread with butter these buns are superb, but if you have a tendency towards indigestion you should probably wait until they have cooled!

1 lb (450g) wholewheat flour
1 tablespoon instant dried yeast
½ teaspoon cinnamon
½ teaspoon ground nutmeg
½ teaspoon mixed spice
4 oz (110g) sultanas
Grated rind of 1 orange
½ teaspoon sea salt
1 tablespoon honey
2 oz (50g) butter or margarine
¼ pint (150ml) warm milk
¼ pint (150ml) warm water
Beaten egg

Mix the flour, yeast, spices, fruit and salt in a large bowl. Dissolve the honey and butter in the milk and water and pour into the flour. Mix well and leave to rise in a warm place for twenty minutes until doubled in size.

Knead, form into 8 balls and flatten each slightly in the palm of your hand. Beat the egg in a shallow bowl and dip in the top of each roll to glaze. Place on a well-oiled tray and leave to rise for another twenty minutes until doubled in size again.

Meanwhile, preheat the oven to Gas Mark 7 (425°F/220°C). Bake 5 minutes then turn the oven down to Gas Mark 6 (400°F/200°C) and bake for a further 15-20 minutes until golden-brown and hollow sounding.

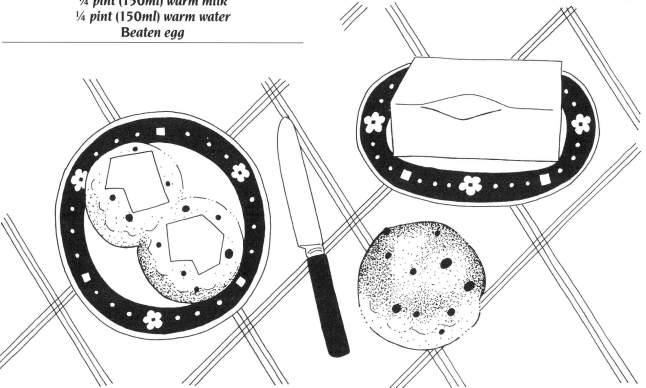

RYE BREAD

10 oz (275g) wholewheat flour
10 oz (275g) strong wholewheat flour (i.e., supermarket bread flour)
1 tablespoon caraway seeds
2 tablespoons instant dried yeast
Grated rind of an orange
1 dessertspoon molasses
1 dessertspoon honey
1 teaspoon sea salt
1 pint (570ml) warm water
12 oz (350g) rye flour

Mix the two wholewheat flours, caraway seeds, yeast, rind, molasses, honey, salt and warm water in a large bowl. Stir well and mix in the rye flour. Cover the bowl with a tea-towel and leave to rise in a warm place for two hours.

Knead well, form into 2 loaves and dust with flour. Press into well-oiled bread tins, tip out and then put them back the other way up. Leave to rise 20-30 minutes until the loaves have almost reached the top of the tins.

Meanwhile, preheat the oven to Gas Mark 4 (350°F/180°C). Bake for 1 hour and glaze the loaves as soon as they are out of the oven with a wet brush dipped in honey.

CHEDDAR AND PARSLEY LOAF
(For 1 loaf)

1 teaspoon molasses
1 teaspoon honey
½ pint (275ml) hand-hot water
14 oz-1 lb (400-450g) wholewheat flour
1 tablespoon instant, dried yeast
4 oz (110g) grated mature Cheddar cheese
1 dessertspoon olive oil
2 tablespoons fresh parsley, chopped fine
¼ teaspoon ground mustard
½ teaspoon sea salt
1 tablespoon sesame seeds

Dissolve the molasses and honey in the warm water in a large bowl. Stir in three-quarters of the flour, plus the yeast, grated cheese, olive oil, parsley, ground mustard and sea salt. Mix well, then leave to rise in a warm place for 30 minutes or until doubled in size.

Punch down and add as much flour as necessary to make a stiff dough. Tip onto a floured board and knead until firm. Form into a loaf.

Oil a large loaf tin and sprinkle the sesame seeds over the bottom. Push the loaf into the tin, fold upwards, and pummel down. Tip out and replace other way up, so the sesame seed covered side becomes the top. Leave to rise a second time in a warm place for twenty minutes or until risen to the top of the tin.

Meanwhile pre-heat the oven to Gas Mark 6 (400°F/200°C). Bake 40 minutes. To test, tip the loaf out of the tin and tap the base. It should sound hollow. If you like, you can leave it to bake out of the tin for 5 minutes more to give a crisp crust.

HOT GARLIC BREAD

The smell of garlic permeates the chopping board, knife, hands and finally the bread. It turns a slightly stale loaf into a buttery, hot feast.

3-5 cloves of garlic (depending on desired potency)
Sea salt
6 oz (175g) butter or margarine at room temperature
1 loaf of bread

Preheat the oven to Gas Mark 6 (400°F/200°C).

Crush and chop the garlic with a little salt and mix well with the softened butter or margarine. Slice the loaf all the way through and spread each slice on both sides with the garlic butter.

Reconstruct the loaf, wrap in foil and bake for 20-30 minutes. Serve hot and steaming.

NUT BREAD
(For 1 loaf)

This is a nutty, moist honey bread, that needs nothing more than a spread of butter.

¼ pint (150ml) milk
1½ tablespoons honey
¼ pint (150ml) hand-hot water
1 dessertspoon olive oil
3oz (75g) walnuts, or a mixture of walnuts and cashews
1 lb (450g) wholewheat flour
½ teaspoon sea salt
1 tablespoon instant, dried yeast

Scald the milk (i.e., heat until it is just about to boil), then dissolve in the honey and stir in the water and oil. Leave to cool to lukewarm.

Chop the nuts fairly small and mix with three quarters of the flour, the salt and the yeast in a large bowl. Make a well in the centre, pour in the liquids and mix thoroughly. Leave to rise in a warm place for 30 minutes or so until doubled in size.

Mix in the rest of the flour, tip out onto a well floured surface and knead until firm. Form into a loaf, place in a well-oiled tin and leave to rise again for 20-30 minutes.

Meanwhile pre-heat the oven to Gas Mark 6 (400°F/200°C). Bake for 40-50 minutes. To test, tip the loaf out of its tin and tap the bottom — it should sound hollow. When it is out of the oven, brush the top of the loaf with honey to glaze and leave to cool on a wire cooling rack.

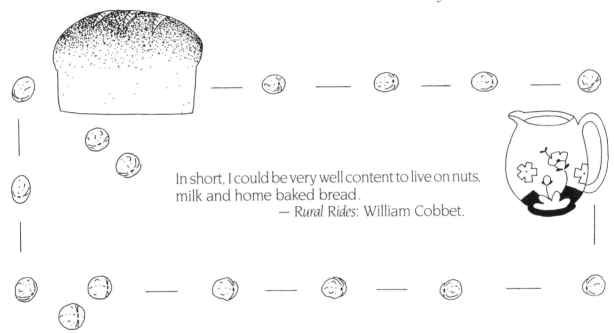

In short, I could be very well content to live on nuts, milk and home baked bread.
— *Rural Rides*: William Cobbet.

FRESH YEAST BREAD
For 2 large loaves

1 dessertspoon honey
2 oz (50g) fresh yeast
1 pint warm water
2 lb (900g) wholewheat flour and extra for flouring the board and hands
1 teaspoon sea salt
1 tablespoon oil

Stir the honey and yeast into half the water in a medium sized bowl. Leave in a warm place for 15 minutes until it is frothy. Mix the flour and salt in a large bowl, then stir in the yeast mixture, oil and the rest of the water. Leave to rise in a warm place for 40 minutes until doubled in size. Tip out onto a well-floured board, dust your hands with flour and knead until firm. Divide into two loaves and roll both in flour. Oil the loaf tins well, press a loaf into each, then tip them out and replace the other way up. (This gives the loaves a good shape.)

Score the tops two or three times with a knife.

Preheat the oven to Gas Mark 6 (400°F/200°C).

Leave the loaves to rise in a warm place for 30 minutes until they have reached the tops of the tins. Bake 40-50 minutes. To test, tip out of the tins and tap the bottoms. They should sound hollow. Leave to cool upside-down or on a wire cooling rack.

SOUPS

I live on good soup not on fine words. — *Moliere.*

There are so many different types of soups — they can be clear, creamed or chunky, thin for starters or thick for a full meal. Milk, tomatoes, potatoes or pulses thicken a soup and a liquidizer creams one. Miso makes a lovely clear soup and is definitely an ingredient to become familiar with, if you're not already.

The Stockpot

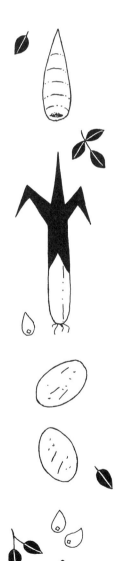

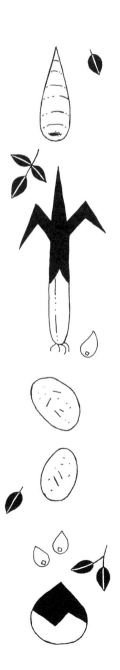

The Café's soups usually start with the stockpot. This sits in the middle of the kitchen floor during the morning's cooking and is filled with everybody's discarded carrot tops, vegetable peelings, cauliflower leaves and such like. In the afternoon it is all simmered for half an hour or so and then the resulting liquid is strained off for the next day's use. Vegetable cooking water can be saved for stock too, particularly potato water. Chickpea and haricot bean water is also very good, but only if the beans have been pre-soaked and the soaking water thrown away. There is usually fierce competition for any such stock. Perhaps someone will need just a little to moisten a rice and vegetable bake, someone else a little for a gravy and yet another will want some for a lasagne sauce; but it is the soupmaker who has unquestioned priority. A stock is often essential to a soup, bringing depth and richness of taste.

If, for some reason, a stock has not been made there is always a jar of natural vegetable stock cubes up amongst the jars on the herb shelf. Dissolved in hot water they make an instant and reasonably tasty stock — useful, but not comparable to the freshly made stuff; so we do encourage you to save your cooking water and vegetable peelings.

Seasonings *Salt really does make a difference, and if your soup is tasting insipid, a pinch may be all that's needed to bring out the flavour. Herbs have a similar effect, and add their own flavours too. And most soups are enhanced by some sort of garnish just before serving — chopped parsley or watercress, a spoonful of cream or yogurt, or toasted sesame seeds.*

CREAM OF ARTICHOKE SOUP

A creamy, thick soup with the lovely, smoky flavour of artichokes.

2 lb (900g) Jerusalem artichokes
1 tablespoon olive oil
½ pint (275ml) stock
1½ pints (850ml) milk
Squeeze of lemon juice
Sea salt and freshly ground black pepper

Scrub the artichokes, chop roughly and sauté for a few minutes in the oil. Add the stock and milk and simmer gently until the artichokes are tender.

Cool a little and liquidize; then reheat, adding the lemon juice if you wish, and seasoning with salt and pepper.

There are soups which can heal all ills. I remember one lunchtime up in the Café office when all the grimness of a V.A.T. return, accounts and a headache was dissolved into creamy bliss by a bowl of artichoke soup.

FASOLADA

6 oz (175g) haricot beans, soaked overnight and drained
2-3 pints (1-2 litres) stock
2 large onions
2 cloves of garlic
2 carrots
3 sticks of celery
3-4 tablespoons olive oil
3 teaspoons tomato purée
2 tablespoons fresh parsley, chopped fine
Sea salt and freshly ground black pepper
1 wine glass red wine

Bring the haricot beans to the boil in the stock then simmer for half an hour.

Dice the onion, garlic, celery and carrot fine and sauté for 10 minutes in half the oil. Add to the beans with the tomato purée, half the parsley and the rest of the olive oil. Continue to simmer until it is all really tender.

Season and stir in the remaining parsley and the red wine, just before serving.

GREEN VEGETABLE SOUP

1 onion
1 tablespoon olive oil
½ teaspoon ground cumin
1 cauliflower
8 oz (225g) spring cabbage
1½ pints (850ml) stock
8 oz (225g) broccoli
2 teaspoons tamari
Sea salt and freshly ground black pepper
Freshly grated nutmeg
Yogurt, to taste

Dice the onion and sauté in the oil with the cumin until soft. Chop the cauliflower and spring cabbage roughly, and add to the onion. Stir and sauté for 5 minutes, then add the stock and simmer.

Chop the broccoli florets and stalks into very small pieces and steam in a colander above the soup until just tender. Put to one side.

Liquidize the other vegetables when they are soft. Reheat and add the broccoli pieces. Stir in the tamari and season with salt, pepper and a little nutmeg. Serve with a generous garnish of yogurt.

CREAM OF CARROT SOUP

2 lb (900g) new-season carrots
1 tablespoon corn oil
½ pint (275ml) stock
1½ pints (850ml) milk
1 teaspoon basil
½ teaspoon caraway seeds (optional)
Squeeze of lemon juice
Sea salt and freshly ground black pepper
Chopped fresh parsley
Sesame seeds

Chop the carrots roughly and sauté in the oil for 5 minutes or so. Add the stock and enough milk to cover and simmer gently until very tender.

Allow to cool a little and then liquidize with the rest of the milk.

Return to the pan and reheat with the basil, caraway seeds and lemon juice. Season to taste.

Garnish with chopped parsley or a sprinkle of sesame seeds.

SIX VEGETABLE SOUP

4 lb (2 kg) mixed vegetables of different textures and colours (see note)
1 teaspoon oregano
1 teaspoon marjoram
Sea salt and freshly ground black pepper
2 pints (115ml) good stock

Layer all the vegetables except cabbage in the soup pot, seasoning with herbs and salt and pepper as you go.

Cover with stock and simmer gently until everything is very tender. Add cabbage in the last 10 minutes of cooking.

Be careful when stirring and serving so as not to lose the shapes of the vegetables.

Note: Marrow and cabbage are essential to this soup but the other vegetables are up to you. The following list is therefore just a suggestion:

Marrow, cut into thin slices
Potatoes, sliced thin
Red and green peppers, sliced into rings
Carrots, sliced into sticks
Cabbage, shredded fine
Artichokes, sliced thin
Onions, sliced into rounds
Celery, sliced into thin lengths
Leeks, sliced into thin lengths

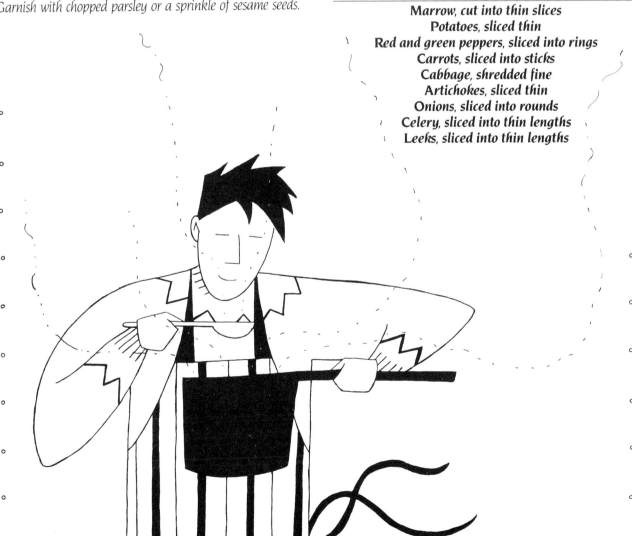

CREAM OF CAULIFLOWER SOUP

1 large cauliflower
4 sticks of celery
1 tablespoon olive oil
1 pint (570ml) milk
½-1 pint (275-570ml) stock
1 teaspoon dill leaves
Sea salt and freshly ground black pepper
Watercress

Chop the cauliflower and celery roughly and sauté in the olive oil for a few minutes without browning.

Add the milk and stock and simmer for 20 minutes until the vegetables are tender.

Cool and liquidize, adding a little more milk or stock as necessary.

Return to heat, add the dill and season with salt and pepper.

Garnish with a few chopped watercress leaves.

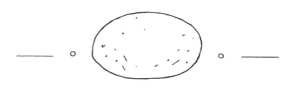

Leeks are notoriously difficult to clean, but there is an infallible method!

Top and tail, cutting away the very tough outer leaves. Slice deeply through to the middle and down the whole length of each leek. Wash under the tap with plenty of cold water, and now each leaf can be opened out separately and all the dirt cleaned away.

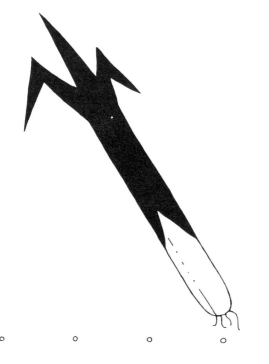

LEEK AND POTATO SOUP

2 lb (900g) leeks
1 lb (450g) potatoes
1 tablespoon vegetable oil
2 pints (1150ml) stock/milk mixture
Freshly grated nutmeg
Sea salt and freshly ground black pepper
Sour cream
Chopped chives

Slice the leeks roughly and dice the potatoes.

Sauté in the oil for 5 minutes and then add the stock and milk.

Cook gently until the potatoes are falling slightly and the leeks are tender. Cool a little and liquidize all or part of the soup.

Reheat and season with nutmeg, salt and pepper.

Garnish with sour cream and chopped fresh chives.

POTATO AND GOMASIO SOUP

1 onion
2 sticks celery
1 lb (450g) potatoes
2 tablespoons olive oil or butter
1 pint (570ml) stock
1 pint (570ml) milk
Sea salt and freshly ground black pepper
1 teaspoon marjoram
Yogurt
Gomasio (see page 54)

Dice the onion and celery. Chop the potatoes roughly. Sauté the onion in the oil or butter until soft. Add the potatoes and celery and sauté 5-10 minutes more. Add the stock and simmer gently until the potato is very tender.

Cool a little and liquidize with the milk. Add the marjoram, season with salt and pepper and simmer for a further 10 minutes.

Serve garnished with yogurt and a generous sprinkling of gomasio.

hot soup ∘ hot soup ∘ hot soup ∘ hot soup ∘

TOMATO SOUP

2 lb (900g) tomatoes (or 2 large tins)
2 medium onions
1 tablespoon olive oil
6 oz (175g) red lentils
2 pints (1150ml) stock
1 teaspoon basil
1 teaspoon marjoram
1 tablespoon fresh parsley, chopped fine
Sea salt and freshly ground black pepper
1 tablespoon butter (optional)
Grated cheese (optional)

If you are using fresh tomatoes, put them into a bowl and pour boiling water over them. Leave for a few minutes, then drain, peel and chop roughly. Dice the onions and sauté in the oil until soft. De-grit the lentils and add to the onion with the tomatoes and stock. Simmer gently for 30-40 minutes until everything is well cooked.

Cool a little and liquidize. Stir in the herbs and butter and season with salt and pepper. Simmer for 10 minutes more.

Garnish with grated cheese or serve with slices of cheese on toast.

LENTIL SOUP

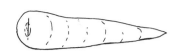

½ an onion
3 sticks celery
1 small turnip
2 carrots
2 cloves garlic
2 tablespoons olive oil
8 oz (225g) red lentils
2 pints (1150ml) stock
1 teaspoon marjoram
1-2 tablespoons fresh parsley, chopped fine
Juice of ½ a lemon
Sea salt and freshly ground black pepper

Dice the onion, celery, turnip, carrots and crush and chop the garlic.

Sauté the onion and garlic in the olive oil until soft. Add the other vegetables and stir and sauté for 10 minutes more.

De-grit the lentils and add to the pot with the stock. Simmer gently until the lentils are well cooked.

Stir in the herbs and lemon juice and season with salt and pepper.

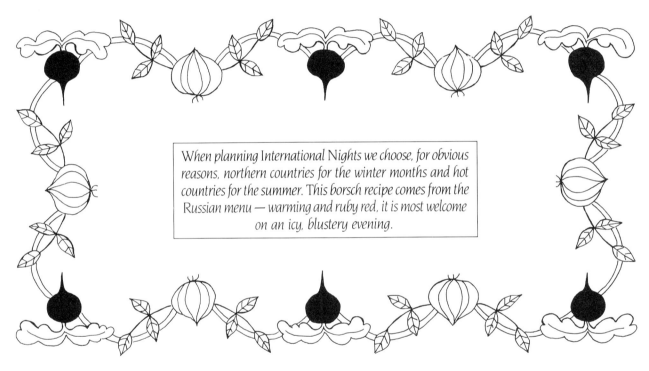

When planning International Nights we choose, for obvious reasons, northern countries for the winter months and hot countries for the summer. This borsch recipe comes from the Russian menu — warming and ruby red, it is most welcome on an icy, blustery evening.

BORSCH

Beetroot takes a long time to cook — about 1½ hours — so this is a good time to make bread, while the beetroot pot is steadily bubbling and warming in the kitchen.

1 lb (450g) beetroot
2 onions
2 carrots
2 sticks celery
1 tablespoon butter
1 teaspoon dill leaves
Squeeze of lemon juice
Yogurt and watercress

Top and tail the beetroot and cut any large ones in half. Wash, but don't try to peel until cooked, when the peel just slides off. Boil gently in 1½ pints (850ml) water until tender.

Drain and reserve the water. Roughly chop the onions, carrots and celery. Peel and cube the beetroot. Sauté the onion in the butter until soft. Add the carrots and celery and sauté for 5 minutes more. Add the beetroot and beetroot water and let it all simmer for 20 minutes or so.

Cool a little, then liquidize. Stir in the dill leaves and lemon juice and add stock to bring to the desired consistency. Reheat and season with salt and pepper.

Serve garnished with yogurt and chopped watercress.

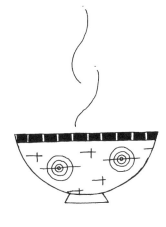

Miso is a Japanese product made from fermented soya beans, very nourishing and renowned for its healing properties.

There are several varieties. The most commonly found are Genmai, made from soya beans and brown rice, Mugi, made from soya beans and barley, and Hatcho, made from soya beans alone. All have a rich, savoury taste. Genmai and Mugi are mellower and milder than the Hatcho and so are probably the best to try first.

Miso should be creamed in a little water and then added to the pot or casserole at the end of the cooking. But never let it boil, as this destroys much of its nutritional value.

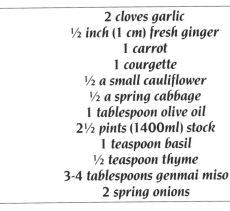

MISO SOUP

The vegetables in this soup can be varied according to what is in season. Green beans, peas, parsnips, swede and mushrooms are all especially good.

2 cloves garlic
½ inch (1 cm) fresh ginger
1 carrot
1 courgette
½ a small cauliflower
½ a spring cabbage
1 tablespoon olive oil
2½ pints (1400ml) stock
1 teaspoon basil
½ teaspoon thyme
3-4 tablespoons genmai miso
2 spring onions

Dice the garlic and ginger fine. Slice the carrot into matchsticks and the courgette into rings or half rings. Chop the cauliflower into very small florets, cutting away the inner stalk and shred the spring cabbage. It is most important that everything is chopped attractively and small.

Sauté all of the vegetables except the spring cabbage in the olive oil for a few minutes. Add the stock and herbs and simmer until everything is almost tender. Add the cabbage, simmer for 5 minutes more and switch off the heat. Mix the miso to a cream in a cup of cold water and stir into the soup.

Serve garnished with chopped spring onion.

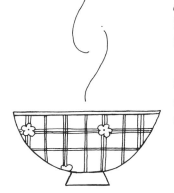

FRENCH ONION SOUP

2 lb (900g) onions
2 oz (50g) butter
1 oz (25g) wholewheat flour
2 pints (1150ml) stock
1 small glass of sherry
Tamari, to taste
Sea salt and freshly ground black pepper
Grated Parmesan
Stale wholewheat bread for croûtons

Slice the onions into thin rings and sauté gently in the butter for 20 minutes until they are a deep golden-brown. Add the flour and cook for a few minutes more, stirring all the while.

Gradually stir in the stock, then the sherry and simmer for 30 minutes or so. Add tamari, salt and pepper to taste.

Serve with plenty of parmesan and croûtons.

Let onion atoms lurk within the bowl.
And, scarce suspected, animate the whole.

— *The Reverend Sydney Smith.*

To make **croûtons**, remove the crust from the bread and cut into ½ inch (1 cm) cubes. Fry in hot oil until golden and crisp.

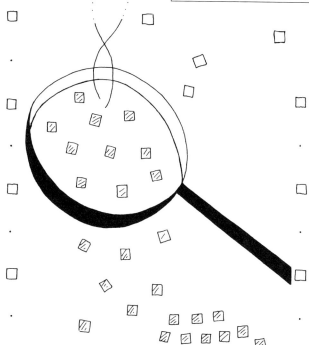

GREEN SPLIT PEA SOUP

If for some reason, as is often the case, the morning's cooking has been hectic — pies and bread just made, salads still in the making and the soup not yet decided on — a split pea soup is often the solution. It is a very good standby when something fast and reliable is needed. And it is an excellent soup in its own right, the rich taste of the peas complimented by the fresh mint; and all a beautiful green.

10 oz (275g) green split peas
1 tablespoon olive oil or butter
3 pints (1700ml) stock
1 tablespoon fresh mint, chopped fine
Dash of tamari
Sea salt and freshly ground black pepper

Sauté the split peas in the oil or butter for a few minutes; add stock and simmer until the peas are completely mushy. Add extra stock as necessary to bring to desired consistency. Stir in the mint and season with tamari, salt and pepper.

A swirl of yogurt or cream as a garnish sets off the green of this soup most attractively.

CLEAR MUSHROOM SOUP

8 oz (175g) button mushrooms
1 clove garlic
1 tablespoon olive oil
2 pints (1140ml) water
1 tablespoon fresh parsley, chopped fine
3 tablespoons genmai miso
Juice of ½ a lemon

Slice the mushrooms and dice the garlic. Sauté in the olive oil for a minute or so. Add the water and parsley and simmer for 5 minutes until the mushrooms are tender.

Mix the miso to a paste in a cup with a little cold water and add to the pan with lemon juice to taste.

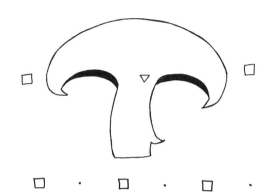

CREAM OF MUSHROOM SOUP

1 small potato
1 lb (450g) button mushrooms
1-2 tablespoons olive oil or butter
½ pint (275ml) stock
1½ pints (850ml) milk
Freshly grated nutmeg
Sea salt and freshly ground black pepper

Peel and dice the potato small. Slice 2 oz (50g) of the mushrooms thinly and put to one side. Chop the rest roughly and sauté with the potato in the butter or oil for 10 minutes.

Add stock and enough milk to cover and simmer gently for half an hour or until the potato is well cooked and is breaking up.

Allow to cool a little, then liquidize with the milk to bring to the consistency of single cream. Return to the pan and add the thinly sliced mushrooms.

Simmer for 10 minutes and season with nutmeg, salt and pepper.

SALADS, DIPS AND PÂTÉS

Devilish good dinner — cold, but capital.
— *Pickwick Papers*: Charles Dickens.

Every Thursday a Café worker takes a barrow to the Leeds markets a few streets away to do the week's buying. There are rows upon rows of stalls, indoors and outdoors, displaying fruit and vegetables of all different colours, shapes and sizes. The buying list starts with the basic vegetables — sacks of potatoes, onions, carrots, cabbages and boxes of lettuce, tomatoes and cucumbers. Then there are the seasonal buys, such as new potatoes in spring, blackberries in the summer, Cox's Orange Pippins in autumn and Brussels sprouts in winter. And there are always some exotic treats for the week's International Night — fresh coriander, yams and maybe a mango.

On the way back, the barrow, now weighed down and piled high, can be quite treacherous. It must be pushed slowly and steadily and this requires great determination on the two busy roads between the market and the Café. Then the barrow is parked in the archway and everything is unloaded into the stockroom. Meanwhile the cooks nip out of the kitchen to take the first pickings and the sudden choice is probably most appreciated by the day's saladmaker. Faced with boxes of cress, white button mushrooms, deep red peppers, heads of crisp celery, scarlet red cabbages and new orange carrots, all sorts of salad possibilities come to mind.

Three different salads are made every day at the Café. By Wednesday the choice in the vegetable stockroom has dwindled; but a grain can always be put on to cook, there are usually beans in soak and what vegetables there are will be used well; for good salads can be made from almost any vegetable, pulse or grain.

Careful chopping makes the most mundane ingredients interesting. Salads usually look nicer if they are chopped fine and small, and this makes them easier to eat, too. Don't limit yourself to slices, but chop in chunks and cubes as well, watching the different sizes, shapes and colours of all the vegetables you're using, matching and contrasting them.

The patés in this section can all be used as a spread, or served with thin slices of toast or vegetable crudités as a starter. The mix of soft and crisp is delicious.

31

CABBAGE AND CURRANT COLESLAW

½ head white cabbage
2 oz (50g) currants
1 teaspoon basil
2-3 tablespoons mayonnaise (see page 52)
Sea salt and freshly ground black pepper

Dice the cabbage very small and stir in the currants, basil and mayonnaise. Season with salt and pepper.

SAVOY, NUT AND APPLE

1 red apple
Juice of ½ lemon
4 sticks celery
½ head savoy cabbage
2 oz (50g) redskin peanuts
2 tablespoons vinaigrette (see page 51)
Sea salt and freshly ground black pepper

Halve, quarter and core the apple and dice into the salad bowl. Pour the lemon juice over it and stir well (this prevents the apple from turning brown).

Dice the celery, and chop the cabbage fine, discarding any tough, outer leaves. Mix everything together with the vinaigrette and season with salt and pepper.

There is a high shelf above one of the kitchen work surfaces where all of the dried herbs and spices are kept, each in an old jam jar and all cluttered behind and on top of each other. And when cooking time is running short, it can take real determination to find a particular one, reaching over other cooks' heads to sort through the jars, first at one end of the shelf, then at the other, often finding it at last on someone else's chopping board. But such a search can be crucial to a recipe.

RED CABBAGE SALAD

The caraway seeds make this salad of red cabbage, carrot and mayonnaise particularly delicious.

3 carrots
½ head red cabbage
1 teaspoon caraway seeds
3 tablespoons mayonnaise (see page 52)
Sea salt and freshly ground black pepper

Dice the carrots and red cabbage very small. (Always use a stainless steel knife when chopping red cabbage as other metals turn the rich, red colour to a blueish purple.)

Stir in the caraway seeds and mayonnaise; season with salt and pepper.

ITALIAN GREEN SALAD

It often happens that someone has to run over to the Leeds markets after breakfast to buy a new box of lettuce; for lettuce can't be stored long. A crisp, green salad compliments the look and taste of any main meal.

This is a very good accompaniment to any pasta dish. Traditionally it is eaten after the main meal on the same plate in the left-over sauces.

1 large lettuce
1 clove garlic
2 tablespoons vinaigrette (see page 51)

Wash the lettuce and drain well. Break up the larger leaves and leave the smaller ones whole. Rub the garlic clove around a large salad bowl and discard.

Put in the lettuce leaves and toss in the vinaigrette just before serving.

LETTUCE AND FLAGEOLET SALAD

3 oz (75g) flageolet beans, soaked overnight
1-2 tablespoons lemon vinaigrette (see page 51)
1 large lettuce
1 box cress
2 tablespoons fresh parsley, chopped fine
Sea salt and freshly ground black pepper

Cook the flageolet beans until tender and drain. Stir a tablespoon of vinaigrette into them while still warm, and leave to cool.

Wash, drain and break up the lettuce. Cut the cress from the box and wash. Mix everything with the beans, stir in another tablespoon of vinaigrette, season and serve.

LETTUCE, MUSHROOM AND SUNFLOWER SEED

1 large lettuce
1 bunch watercress
4 oz (100g) button mushrooms
2 tablespoons vinaigrette (see page 51)
2 oz (50g) toasted sunflower seeds (see page 54)
Sea salt and freshly ground black pepper

Wash, drain and break up the lettuce. Roughly chop the watercress leaves and slice the mushrooms thinly, keeping any very small ones whole. Toss everything together in the vinaigrette, season, sprinkle with sunflower seeds and serve.

CAULIFLOWER SALAD

1 small cauliflower
1 carrot
½ cucumber
1 box cress
1 teaspoon poppyseeds
1 teaspoon basil
Yogurt dressing (see page 54)
Sea salt and freshly ground black pepper

Cut away the outer, dark green leaves of the cauliflower but keep the tender, new ones. Chop and dice thoroughly. Dice the carrot very small and dice the cucumber. Cut the cress from the box and wash.

Toss everything together with the poppyseeds, basil and dressing. Season.

33

FENNEL SALAD

1 head Chinese leaves
1 small fennel bulb
3 oz (75g) walnuts
1 teaspoon dill leaves
2 tablespoons lemon vinaigrette (see page 51)
Sea salt and freshly ground black pepper

Shred the Chinese leaves and slice the fennel thinly. Roughly chop the walnuts. Mix everything together and stir in the dill leaves and vinaigrette. Season.

CARROT SALAD

4 large carrots
3 oz (75g) currants
3-4 tablespoons orange juice

Wash, scrape and grate the carrots. Stir in the currants and orange juice.

CARROT AND PARSNIP SALAD

2 large carrots
2 large parsnips
3-4 tablespoons orange juice

Wash and scrape the carrots, peel the parsnips and chop both into large chunks. Next grate the pieces of carrot and parsnip alternately into the salad bowl. (This is the best way to mix the two together.) Pour the orange juice over and stir.

BEETROOT SALAD

A very beautiful salad, the deep red of the beetroot turning pink in the yogurt.

2 lb (900g) beetroot
½ teaspoon dill leaves
2 tablespoons yogurt
Sea salt and freshly ground black pepper

Top and tail the beetroot and cook until tender. Cool, peel and dice fairly large. Mix the dill leaves into the yogurt and pour over the beetroot. Stir and season.

POTATO SALAD

2 lb (900g) potatoes
4 tablespoons mayonnaise (see page 52)
A few watercress leaves
Sea salt and freshly ground black pepper

Choose a firm type of potato such as Majestic, King Edward or Desirée. Cook the potatoes gently until tender. Drain, chop into chunks and mix with the mayonnaise and chopped watercress leaves. Season and cool.

NEW POTATO SALAD

There is nothing quite like new potatoes and fresh mint . . .

1½ lbs (700g) new potatoes
2-3 tablespoons vinaigrette (see page 51)
1 bunch of fresh mint leaves, chopped
Sea salt and freshly ground black pepper

Halve or quarter the large potatoes and leave the small ones whole. Cook and drain. Stir in the vinaigrette, chopped mint and seasoning while the potatoes are still warm.

RICE SALAD

8 oz (225g) long-grain brown rice
2 bay leaves
18 fl oz (500ml) water
Sea salt and freshly ground black pepper
¼ cucumber
3 oz (75g) button mushrooms
½ red pepper
3 oz (75g) redskin peanuts
1 tablespoon fresh parsley, chopped fine
2-3 tablespoons lemon vinaigratte (see page 51)

Cook the rice with the bay leaves, water and a pinch of salt in a saucepan with a tight-fitting lid until all of the water has been absorbed and the rice is tender.

Drain in a colander and rinse some cold water through, as this keeps the grains separate. Remove the bayleaves and cool.

Dice the cucumber, slice the mushrooms thinly and chop the red pepper into very small pieces. Mix it all into the rice with the peanuts and parsley. Season and stir in the vinaigrette.

TABOULEH

A traditional salad from the Middle East based on bulgur, fresh parsley and fresh mint. Bulgur is a cracked wheat grain, available in most wholefood shops, which is very simple and quick to cook.

8 oz (225g) bulgur wheat
3 tomatoes
2 tablespoons fresh parsley, chopped fine
1 tablespoon fresh mint, chopped fine
1 garlic clove
2-3 tablespoons lemon vinaigrette (see page 51)
Sea salt and freshly ground black pepper

Pour just enough boiling water over the bulgur to cover it. Leave for 30-45 minutes until the bulgur has soaked up all the water and is light and soft, but chewy.

Chop the tomato into smallish chunks and stir into the bulgur with the chopped parsley and mint. Crush the garlic, add to the vinaigrette and pour over the salad. Season.

TOMATO AND BASIL SALAD

A salad from an aunt in Italy, where fresh basil abounds. Sadly, it doesn't grow well in Britain, but if you do come by some, this simple combination shows it at its best.

Otherwise fresh mint is a good alternative.

1 lb (450g) tomatoes
1 bunch fresh basil leaves chopped
1 tablespoon olive oil
Sea salt and freshly ground black pepper

Slice the tomatoes into thin rounds and place on a large plate. Scatter the chopped basil leaves over the tomato rounds, pour on the olive oil and season.

TOMATO AND CUCUMBER SALAD

5 firm tomatoes
½ cucumber
4 oz (110g) black olives
1 tablespoon fresh parsley, chopped fine
1 tablespoon lemon vinaigrette (see page 51)
Sea salt and freshly ground black pepper

Cut the tomatoes into smallish chunks and dice the cucumber into similar sized pieces. Mix with the olives, parsley and vinaigrette. Season.

CUCUMBER AND YOGURT SALAD

A cooling raita for a curry, or a salad to go with anything.

1 cucumber
½ teaspoon dill leaves
Sea salt
2 tablespoons yogurt

Slice the cucumber into very thin rounds. Mix the dill and a little salt into the yogurt and pour over the cucumber.

WALDORF SALAD

A salad for the autumn when the shops are full of Cox's, Russets and new celery.

3 apples
Juice of 1 lemon
½ head celery
4 oz (110g) walnuts
4 oz (110g) dates
2 tablespoons mayonnaise (see page 52)

Core the apples, dice and soak in the lemon juice. Chop the celery and roughly chop the walnuts and dates.

Mix with the mayonnaise.

35

WHEAT SALAD

The chewy texture of wheat grain makes a very good basis for a salad. It has a slightly sweet flavour which is offset here by a yogurt dressing and caraway seeds.

6 oz (175g) whole wheat grain
2 carrots
1 red apple
Juice of ½ lemon
½ cucumber
Yogurt dressing (see page 54)
½ teaspoon caraway seeds
1 oz (25g) currants
1 teaspoon basil

Cook the wheat in plenty of water until tender. Drain and leave to cool.

Wash, scrape and grate the carrots. Core the apple, dice and soak in the lemon juice. Dice the cucumber into small chunks.

Mix everything together with the dressing, caraway seeds, currants and basil.

CHICKPEA AND WATERCRESS SALAD

8 oz (225g) chickpeas, soaked overnight
2-3 tablespoons lemon vinaigrette (see page 51)
½ red pepper
1 bunch watercress
1 tablespoon fresh parsley, chopped fine
Sea salt and freshly ground black pepper

Cook the chick peas until tender and drain. Put into the salad bowl, stir in 2 tablespoons of vinaigrette and leave to cool.

Dice the red pepper finely, chop the watercress and mix into the chickpeas with the parsley.

Dress with a little more vinaigrette if you prefer it more moist, and season.

CARROT AND WATERCRESS SALAD

1 carrot
½ cucumber
1 bunch watercress
2 oz (50g) redskin peanuts
½ teaspoon poppyseeds
2 tablespoons tofu dressing (see page 54)
Sea salt and freshly ground black pepper

Dice the carrot finely. Chop the cucumber into small chunks and shred the watercress, discarding any tough stalks. Mix together with the peanuts, poppyseeds and dressing. Season.

GARLIC MUSHROOMS

This dish is usually served as a starter with slices of hot buttered toast. However it is also very good as an accompaniment. Try it with yogurt over steamed spinach or potatoes baked in their jackets and sliced open.

4 large cloves garlic
1 lb (450g) button mushrooms
2 tablespoons butter
Sea salt and freshly ground black pepper

Crush the garlic and slice the mushrooms thinly. Melt the butter in a medium-sized saucepan and fry the garlic for a minute or so. Add the mushrooms and sauté until soft. Season with salt and pepper.

GREEN BEAN AND CAPER SALAD

12 oz (350g) green beans
2-3 tablespoons lemon vinaigrette (see page 51)
Sea salt and freshly ground black pepper
1 tablespoon capers
1 tablespoon fresh parsley, chopped fine

Top and tail the beans and chop into 1 inch (2.5cm) lengths. Steam or boil until just tender. Drain, and while still warm, stir in the vinaigrette, plenty of freshly ground black pepper and a little salt. Chill. Then stir in the capers, a little of the caper liquid and the parsley.

RED AND WHITE BEAN SALAD

4 oz (110g) black eye beans, soaked overnight
4 oz (110g) red kidney beans, soaked overnight
2-3 tablespoons vinaigrette (see page 51)
2 tomatoes
1 box cress
1 teaspoon basil
1 teaspoon black poppyseeds
Sea salt and freshly ground black pepper

Cook the two types of bean separately until tender. Drain and mix in the salad bowl. Stir in 2 tablespoons of vinaigrette and leave to cool.

Dice the tomatoes into small chunks; cut the cress from the box and wash. Stir into the beans with the basil and poppyseeds.

Add a little more vinaigrette if necessary and season.

[Try either of the two previous salads with a sprinkling of tamari-toasted sunflower seeds (see page 54).]

Full o' beans and benevolence.
— Handley Cross: R. S. Surtees.

CRUDITÉS

So many vegetables pass through the Café kitchen to be washed, chopped, cooked, served and eaten that there is a tendency for them to become just a hazy blur to the Café cooks. But crudité making brings back a realization of each vegetable's unique colour and shape. Crudités can be made from all sorts of vegetables:

circles of cucumber, florets of cauliflower sprigs of fresh parsley and mint. slivers of carrot and celery. small whole radishes button mushrooms, trimmed spring onions, thin rings of green and red pepper

Choose and prepare a selection of these and arrange them around
a plate with a pâté in the middle.

PÂTÉS

AVOCADO PÂTÉ

2 ripe avocados
1 tablespoon olive oil
Juice of 1 lemon
Sea salt and freshly ground black pepper

Cut the avocados in half, remove the stones and peel. Mash the flesh with the other ingredients until creamy.

Usually served with crudités or quarters of toast as a starter. Or try it grilled on toast — a very tasty, green version of cheese on toast.

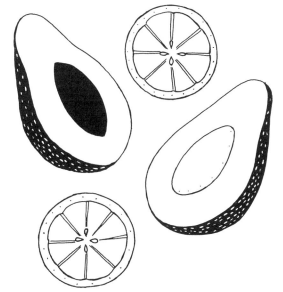

HUMMUS

The Café made huge quantities for a fair stall one summer and borrowed Suma's peanut butter making machine for the mixing. It took about ten minutes to make the hummus but another two hours to clean the machine until it was in a fit state to make peanut butter again! But don't worry, domestic machines don't suffer from the same disadvantages!

A Middle Easten purée of chick peas, tahini, lemon juice and parsley.

8 oz (225g) chickpeas, soaked overnight
3 tablespoons tahini
Juice of 2 lemons
6 tablespoons olive oil
1 tablespoon chopped fresh parsley
2-3 garlic cloves
Sea salt
Paprika and lemon slices to garnish

Cook the chickpeas in plenty of water until very soft. Drain and reserve the cooking water.

Mash the chickpeas to a smooth cream with the tahini, lemon juice, olive oil, and as much chickpea stock as is necessary to bring it to a workable consistency. A liquidizer or vegetable mill helps here if you have one, but if not it can be done by hand though it takes a little longer.

When the mixture is very smooth, stir in the parsley, crushed and chopped garlic and sea salt to taste.

Garnish with a little paprika and lemon slices.

HARICOT AND MINT PÂTÉ

The mint for this pâté is usually picked from the Café's own yard. The herb garden in the yard has had a mixed fortune, depending on whether there have been any garden-minded cooks in the collective or not. In the Café's early years the garden thrived with carefully tended parsley, thyme, mint, marjoram, flowers and shrubs but then fell sadly to weeds as the gardeners left. A year ago another determined gardener joined the Café and immediately set to work on it. It flourished and the Café is full of fresh herbs again, much to the appreciation of all the cooks, even the most city-minded.

**8 oz (225g) haricot beans, soaked overnight
2 tablespoons olive oil
Juice of 1 large lemon
1 tablespoon fresh mint, chopped fine
Sea salt and freshly ground black pepper
Slices of lemon and extra mint leaves to garnish**

Cook the haricot beans until tender. This takes a long time (1-1½ hours), so do watch them and add more water as necessary.

Drain, reserving the cooking water, and cool a little.

Now liquidize with the olive oil, lemon juice and as much of the cooking water as is necessary to give it a workable consistency. Tip into a bowl and mix in the mint, salt and pepper.

Garnish with lemon slices and mint leaves.

AUBERGINE PÂTÉ

The soft, cooked pulp of aubergines lends itself very well to pâté making. It is combined here with tahini, lemon juice and parsley.

**3 medium aubergines
2 tablespoons olive oil
2 tablespoons tahini
2 tablespoons fresh parsley, chopped fine
1 clove garlic
Sea salt and freshly ground black pepper
Juice of half a lemon**

Prick the aubergines with a fork and bake at Gas Mark 5 (375°F/190°C) for 45 minutes until very tender when skewered. Leave to cool a little. Then cut in half, scoop out the flesh and liquidize with the olive oil and tahini. Stir in the parsley and garlic and season with salt, pepper and lemon juice to taste.

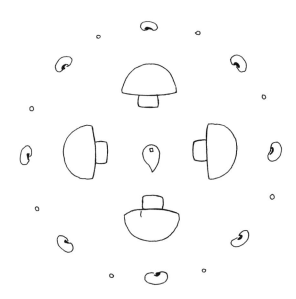

BLACKEYE BEAN AND MUSHROOM PÂTÉ

**8 oz (225g) blackeye beans, soaked overnight
4 oz (110g) mushrooms
1 garlic clove, chopped fine
4 tablespoons olive oil
Juice of 1 large lemon
Sea salt and freshly ground black pepper
Black poppyseeds**

Cook the blackeye beans for half an hour or so until tender. Drain and reserve the stock.

Choose one nice mushroom and slice thinly for a garnish. Chop the other mushrooms roughly and sauté with the garlic in half the olive oil.

Now liquidize the beans and mushrooms with the rest of the olive oil, lemon juice and enough bean stock to bring it to a cream.

Season with salt and pepper, and garnish with the mushroom slices and a sprinkle of poppyseeds.

WALNUT, OLIVE AND TOFU DIP

Tofu is a soya bean curd available in most wholefood shops or Chinese specialist shops. It is high in protein, low in fat and very versatile.

2 oz (50g) olives
2 oz (50g) walnuts
10 oz (275g) tofu
1 tablespoon olive oil
1 teaspoon tamari
Juice of ½ lemon
Freshly ground black pepper

Stone and chop the olives; crush the walnuts. Then liquidize the tofu, olive oil, tamari and lemon juice and stir in the olives, walnuts and a little pepper.

SPINACH AND TOFU PURÉE

1 lb (450g) spinach
1 tablespoon olive oil
Juice of ½ lemon
5 oz (150g) tofu
1 teaspoon tamari
Nutmeg

Wash the spinach well and shred, discarding any tough stalks. Sauté in the olive oil until very soft, then liquidize with the lemon juice, tofu and tamari until creamy. Stir in a little freshly grated nutmeg and serve.

EGG MAYONNAISE

Simple, eggy and crunchy, this dish was brought into the Café by a very enthusiastic American cook.

1 stick of celery
3 red radishes
3 hard-boiled eggs
Mayonnaise (see page 52)
1 tablespoon fresh parsley, chopped fine
Sea salt and freshly ground black pepper
Paprika

Dice the celery finely, slice the radishes and roughly chop the eggs. Mix together in a serving bowl and pour in mayonnaise until it is wet enough to your taste. Stir in the parsley and season with salt and pepper and a pinch of paprika.

42

SAUCES, DRESSINGS AND CONDIMENTS

The Café has recently bought a new six-ring industrial cooker. Colour brochures for such cookers had been looked at and pined over for years, so when the huge, gleaming object finally arrived there was much excitement and celebration. Before its arrival everything was cooked on two small domestic cookers. They were old and worn when they came to the Café and then over-used, so they were usually on the verge of breaking down, and when one or the other did give its last tired puff of gas (in the middle of a morning's cooking) someone would have to rush out to the second-hand shops for a replacement.

We used huge catering pans on these cookers and they had to fight for space on the tiny gas rings. But even in those times, room was always found somewhere for a pan of sauce. Sauces play such an important part in cooking. A hot apple sauce transforms a vegetable and grain bake, as does a gravy over a savoury pie. And there is nothing so simple and delicious as cheese sauce over steamed leeks.

Sauces should be made slowly, watched and stirred through the cooking. A double boiler is best if you have one, but if not a low heat will usually do.

WHITE SAUCE

Wholewheat flour can be used to thicken a sauce just as you would use white flour. It adds a nice nutty flavour and is just a little grainier. But if you prefer a smooth white sauce, use unbleached white flour.

2 tablespoons butter or margarine
2 tablespoons flour
¾-1 pint (425-570ml) milk depending on the required thickness
Sea salt and freshly ground black pepper

Melt the butter, add the flour and stir into a ball (or roux). Stir and cook very gently for a few minutes.

Turn off the heat and add the milk drop by drop, stirring each addition in thoroughly before the next.

When all of the milk has been added, return to the heat and slowly bring to the boil, stirring all the while. Allow to thicken, then season.

flour and butter and flour and butter and flour

Variations:

HERBY WHITE SAUCE

1 small onion
1 tablespoon fresh parsley, chopped fine
1 teaspoon marjoram

Dice the onion small and cook in the butter until soft. Add the flour and continue as usual. Add the herbs after all the milk has been stirred in.

CHEESE SAUCE

2 bay leaves
6 oz (175g) grated Cheddar cheese

Add the bay leaves to the butter with the flour. Stir in the cheese after the milk. Remove the bay leaves before serving.

WATERCRESS SAUCE

1 bunch watercress
Squeeze of lemon juice

Put the watercress into a bowl, pour boiling water over and leave for a minute. Drain and chop fine.

Stir into the sauce after all the milk has been added, and squeeze in a little lemon juice.

LEEK SAUCE

A tasty sauce and very beautiful — light green with flecks of deep green.

2 medium leeks (about 12 oz/350g)
1 small onion
1 tablespoon butter
¼ teaspoon mace

Wash the leeks well (see page 24) and dice, using as much of the green part as is tender. Dice the onion, Sauté both in the butter with the mace until soft. Put half of it into a liquidizer and blend, gradually adding the prepared white sauce. Pour into a saucepan, stir in the unliquidized half, and reheat.

MUSHROOM SAUCE

6 oz (170g) mushrooms
Freshly ground nutmeg

Slice the mushrooms thinly and sauté in the butter until tender before adding the flour.

Grate the nutmeg into the sauce after it has thickened.

BRANDY SAUCE

Dash of brandy
½-1 tablespoon soft raw cane sugar

Stir the brandy and sugar into the sauce to taste and heat through.

BROWN SAUCE ('GRAVY')

2 tablespoons olive oil
2 tablespoons wholewheat flour
1 teaspoon thyme
1 pint (570ml) stock
1 tablespoon shoyu or tamari
Sea salt and freshly ground black pepper

Heat the olive oil, add the flour and thyme, stir and cook for a few minutes.

Gradually add the stock stirring constantly. Bring to the boil and allow to thicken. Add the shoyu or tamari and season with salt and pepper.

Variations:

ONION GRAVY

Sauté a finely diced onion in the olive oil until soft; add the flour and continue as usual.

GRAVY WITH WINE

Reduce 1 glass red wine to half its volume by fast boiling and add to the gravy.

TAMARI AND GINGER SAUCE

A sauce with an oriental flavour — try it with lightly stir-fried vegetables and rice.

1 clove garlic
½ onion
1 inch (2.5cm) fresh ginger
1 tablespoon olive oil
1 pint (570ml) stock or water
1½ tablespoons tamari
2 teaspoons arrowroot

Chop the garlic, onion and ginger finely and sauté in the oil until the onion is tender. Add the stock and tamari and bring to the boil.

Mix the arrowroot to a paste in a little cold water and stir into the sauce. Cook for a few minutes to thicken.

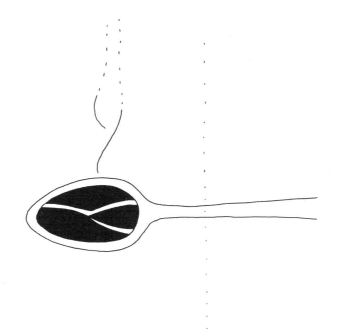

He always aided and comforted me when he could in some way of his own and he always did so at dinnertime by giving me gravy if there were any. There being plenty of gravy today, Joe spooned into my plate at this point, about half a pint.
— *Great Expectations*: Charles Dickens

YOGURT SAUCE

1 onion
1 tablespoon olive oil
1 level teaspoon ground cumin
1 pint (570ml) yogurt

Chop the onion finely and sauté in the olive oil until very soft. Add the cumin and cook a minute or so longer.

Stir in the yogurt and heat very gently. Liquidize if you like and reheat, being careful not to boil.

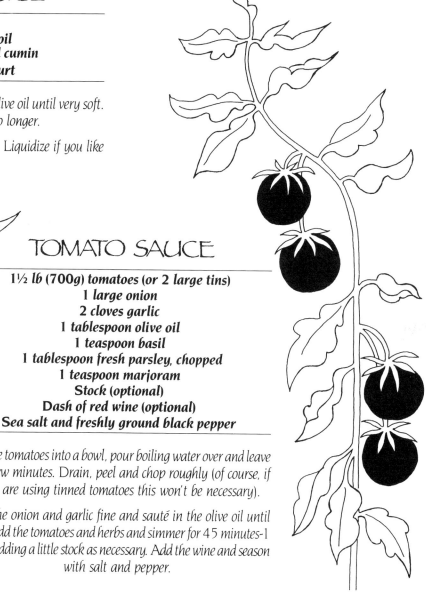

TOMATO SAUCE

1½ lb (700g) tomatoes (or 2 large tins)
1 large onion
2 cloves garlic
1 tablespoon olive oil
1 teaspoon basil
1 tablespoon fresh parsley, chopped
1 teaspoon marjoram
Stock (optional)
Dash of red wine (optional)
Sea salt and freshly ground black pepper

Put the tomatoes into a bowl, pour boiling water over and leave for a few minutes. Drain, peel and chop roughly (of course, if you are using tinned tomatoes this won't be necessary).

Dice the onion and garlic fine and sauté in the olive oil until soft. Add the tomatoes and herbs and simmer for 45 minutes-1 hour, adding a little stock as necessary. Add the wine and season with salt and pepper.

TAHINI SAUCE

Tahini and tamari combine deliciously, making a savoury sauce for steamed vegetables, pies and grains.

4 tablespoons tahini
1 tablespoon tamari
½ pint (275ml) water

Mix the tahini and tamari together in a bowl. Then stir in the water, adding only a little at a time and mixing each addition in well before the next. As the mixture becomes thinner, you will be able to add the remaining water more quickly. Pour into a saucepan and heat gently, stirring all the time and being careful not to boil.

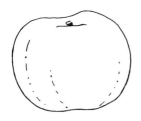
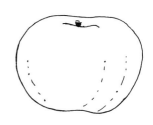

Cooks are notorious for dearly held kitchen beliefs that cause much pain and fury if ever challenged. And Café cooks are no exception. There is heated disagreement over the toast at breakfast, whether it should be thinly or thickly sliced, toasted a light golden or a deep brown. There is disagreement about how big the bread rolls should be, about how much dressing should be poured over the salads, about whether raw onion adds a piquancy to a salad or just indigestibility; about how thickly or moderately a gateau should be spread with cream; and not least, about whether apples should be peeled for making apple sauce!

Despite such arguments the collective members respect each others cooking abilities, and these areas of controversy are coped with on the whole by allowing the cooks free reign in whatever they are cooking each day.

I personally think that an apple sauce should be soft and smooth and so my recipe comes to you with peeled apples; but the choice is yours. Whichever you decide, a Bramley apple sauce will bring a delicious tartness to the pies and main meals you serve it with. The degree of sweetness is again a matter of choice.

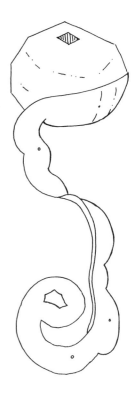

APPLE SAUCE

2 lb (900g) cooking apples, such as Bramleys
2 tablespoons butter (optional)
4 tablespoons water
2 oz (50g) soft raw cane sugar
Squeeze of lemon juice

Peel, core and chop the apples. Cook with the butter and water, stirring with a wooden spoon until it becomes a purée. Stir in the sugar and lemon juice.

Both this and the following Cranberry Sauce can be served as a relish with Nutroast, Potato Bakes or Savoury Pies.

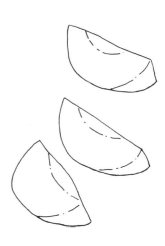

CASHEW CREAM

A luxurious nut cream to serve with desserts and cakes.

4 oz (110g) cashew nuts
3 tablespoons water
4 teaspoons concentrated apple juice

Put the cashews into a liquidizer and whizz with a very little of the water to make a paste. Gradually add the rest of the liquid, alternating water and concentrated apple juice, liquidizing each addition as you go. This makes a fairly thick cream.

Add a little more liquid if you want a pouring consistency.

CRANBERRY SAUCE

8 oz (225g) cranberries
4 fl oz (125ml) water
2-3 oz (50-75g) soft raw cane sugar

Wash the cranberries and remove any stems. Stew in the water until very soft, then beat to a purée. Add sugar to taste and a little more water if necessary to bring to the desired consistency.

SPICED TOFU CREAM

For pouring over fruit salads, cakes or puddings.

8 oz (225g) tofu
1 teaspoon ground cinnamon
1 tablespoon concentrated apple juice
Juice of 1 lemon
½ teaspoon grated nutmeg
½ tablespoon honey

Blend everything in a liquidizer.

STIRRED CUSTARD

2 eggs
1 dessertspoon soft raw cane sugar
A few drops of vanilla essence
½ pint (275ml) milk

Whisk the eggs, sugar and vanilla in a bowl. Heat the milk until it is just beginning to boil, then pour into the eggs, stirring all the while. Strain into a double saucepan, or heavy-bottomed pan and stir over a gentle heat until it thickens. Remove from heat and pour immediately into a sauce jug (otherwise the custard will continue to cook for a little while in the heat of the pan, and may curdle). Serve hot or cold, with stewed fruit, sliced banana, or fruit pies.

oil and vinegar oil and vinegar oil a

DRESSINGS

Economy drives are a common event at the Café, and during one which we held some time ago we decided to use soya oil in salad dressings instead of olive oil. But this was soon surreptitiously 'forgotten' and olive oil poured freely in the kitchen again. For olive oil has a mellow, full flavour, while soya oil is bland, and a dressing should bring flavour to a salad, otherwise all it brings is oiliness.

Dressings really are an area where a little extra expense is well worthwhile. So choose a good quality oil — olive oil or cold pressed corn oil, and a good wine vinegar or fresh lemon juice.

Oil and vinegar are very resistant to each other. They are best combined by a vigorous shake in a jar or bottle with a screw-top lid. Dress vegetable salads just before serving to keep them crisp. Pulses are the exception, however, and should be dressed as soon as they are cooked and drained, as they absorb much more of the dressing's flavour while still warm.

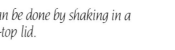

VINAIGRETTE

1 tablespoon wine vinegar
¼ teaspoon mustard powder
3-4 tablespoons olive oil

Mix everything thoroughly. This can be done by shaking in a jar with a screw-top lid.

Variations:

GARLIC VINAIGRETTE

Add 1 clove of garlic, crushed and chopped.

LEMON VINAIGRETTE

Substitute the juice of half a lemon for the vinegar.

TAMARI VINAIGRETTE

Add ½ teaspoon tamari to the vinaigrette. This is particularly good for lettuce or bean salads.

MAYONNAISE

Making mayonnaise by hand is patient, laborious work. If you have the time, it can be quite pleasant, beating oil, drip by drip into an egg and watching the golden mixture turn slowly white. But, if you have limited time and a liquidizer, it can made in a couple of minutes, and this is how it is done at the Café.

---

1 egg
1 dessertspoon wine vinegar
¼ teaspoon ground mustard
¼ teaspoon sea salt
Freshly ground black pepper
Olive oil, corn oil, or a mixture (for the quantity, see below)

Break the egg into a liquidizer with the vinegar, mustard, salt and pepper. Whizz it all together for a few minutes. Pour the oil through the top of the machine, liquidizing all the while. Pour very slowly at first and then more quickly until the mayonnaise is thick.

You will need a lot of oil for this 6-8 fl oz (175-225 ml).

Variations:

LEMON MAYONNAISE

---

1 dessertspoon lemon juice (to replace the vinegar)

Put the lemon juice and egg in the liquidizer and give a short whizz (If the lemon juice and egg are mixed for too long without the oil, the mixture can curdle). Add the oil slowly, as in the basic recipe.

MINT MAYONNAISE

---

1 tablespoon fresh mint, chopped fine

Stir into the prepared mayonnaise.

AÏOLI

A garlic mayonnaise, usually served as a dip for crudités (see page 38).

---

2 or 3 garlic cloves
1 dessertspoon lemon juice (to replace the vinegar)

Crush the garlic cloves and put into the liquidizer with the lemon juice, whizz and then add the egg. Whizz again, very quickly, then slowly add the oil as in the basic recipe.

YOGURT MAYONNAISE

A mixture of one part yogurt to one part mayonnaise makes a lighter, tarter dressing.

HERB MAYONNAISE

½ teaspoon dill leaves
1 tablespoon fresh parsley or fresh chives, or a mixture of both chopped fine

Stir into the prepared mayonnaise.

CARAWAY MAYONNAISE

Caraway seeds have a distinctive sweet yet piquant taste that complements many vegetables — cabbage, potato and carrots in particular.

½ teaspoon caraway seeds

Stir into the prepared mayonnaise.

SOUR CREAM DRESSING

1 tablespoon fresh mint or chives, chopped fine
Squeeze of lemon juice
Pinch of mustard powder
¼ pint (150ml) sour cream
Sea salt and freshly ground black pepper

Stir the mint or chives, lemon juice and mustard powder into the sour cream. Season with salt and pepper.

BLUE CHEESE DRESSING

2 oz (50g) Blue Stilton (at room temperature)
4 fl oz (125ml) yogurt
3 fl oz (75ml) mayonnaise
1 spring onion, diced finely
Sea salt and freshly ground black pepper
Squeeze of lemon juice

Mash the cheese with a fork, then stir in the yogurt, mayonnaise and spring onion. Mix well and season with salt and pepper and a little lemon juice.

TOFU DRESSING

8 oz (225g) tofu
2 tablespoons olive oil
Juice of ½ lemon
1 teaspoon tamari
¼ teaspoon sea salt
1 tablespoon fresh parsley, chopped fine
Freshly ground black pepper

Liquidize the tofu, oil, lemon juice, tamari and salt until creamy. Stir in the parsley and a little pepper and check the seasonings.

YOGURT DRESSING

3 tablespoons yogurt
3 tablespoons olive oil
¼ teaspoon mustard powder
1 tablespoon fresh parsley, chopped fine

Simply mix everything together thoroughly.

CONDIMENTS

TOASTED SUNFLOWER SEEDS

Toast a handful of sunflower seeds in a tray under a grill or in a skillet on the cooker top. Stir and keep a close watch until they turn golden-brown.

They can be eaten as a snack or added to salads and bakes, as can the tamari sunflower seeds.

TAMARI SUNFLOWER SEEDS

These are compulsively delicious. Experience has taught that a batch put aside to cool for a salad should be put well out of reach of passing hands.

2 oz (50g) sunflower seeds
1 teaspoon tamari

Toast the sunflower seeds under the grill or in a skillet until just turning golden, then stir in the tamari.

GOMASIO

This is a sesame salt. Sprinkle it over salads, soups, grains — in fact anywhere you would use salt.

3 tablespoons sesame seeds
1 teaspoon sea salt

Toast the seeds with the salt in a saucepan over a cooker ring. Tip the pan back and forth until the seeds are a deep golden brown, then grind in a surbachi or an electric grinder. It is particularly satisfying to use a surbachi, bursting the seeds open and releasing the aroma slowly, by hand. When the gomasio has cooled, store in an airtight jar.

YOGURT AND GOMASIO

Yogurt and gomasio go beautifully with steamed vegetables, particularly broccoli, leeks or spinach.

Pour a generous spoonful of yogurt over each helping and then sprinkle with plenty of gomasio.

BREADCRUMBS

It is not worthwhile heating the oven specially for breadcrumb-making. Make some when you are doing some other baking.

Break stale bread into small pieces and crumble in a liquidizer, grinder or food processor. Scatter over a baking tray and bake until golden-brown.

Cool and store in an airtight jar.

MAIN MEALS

Once a month the Café takes the barrow to collect supplies from Suma, the wholefood wholesaler in the next street. The barrow is pushed around and past the trucks in the entrance bay and into the warehouse, a large place smelling of dried fruit and wood. The walls are lined with shelves and the floor with pallets, all stacked with sacks and boxes; and the entrance is surrounded by orders piled ready for collection. The Wharf Street order is found and loaded onto the barrow — sacks of rice and beans, boxes of sultanas and figs (which come in attractive wooden boxes which are fought for when empty), bags of hazel and brazil nuts and tubs of honey. Occasionally we would be the happy beneficiaries of a warehouse accident. A box of malt jars was dropped once and one or two jars broke, covering the others in thick, brown stickiness. It wasn't worth the time to wash and relabel them so they were passed on to us, and kept us in malt for months.

The order is wheeled back to the Café and each sack dragged up the stairs to the stock room. Then the sacks are opened and poured into bins and the boxes put up onto shelves. Large glass jars are brought up from the kitchen, filled with pulses, nuts and grains and returned to the kitchen shelf in a line of varied patterns and bright colours.

These wholefoods are combined with fresh vegetables, sauces, eggs, cheeses and yogurt to make many satisfying, tasty meals. You can be sure of sufficient protein in a diet of this sort by mixing foods from at least two of the four vegetarian protein groups: nuts and seeds, pulses, grains, and dairy products; for mixing protein types greatly increases their effectiveness.

The following recipes are a selection from the many main meals made at the Café. They range from the elaborate for when you have the time and inclination to the more simple when you haven't.

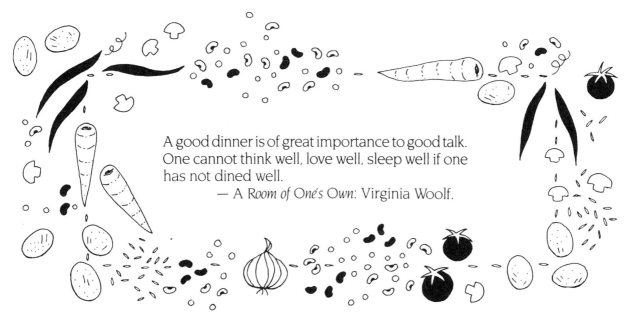

A good dinner is of great importance to good talk. One cannot think well, love well, sleep well if one has not dined well.
— A *Room of One's Own*: Virginia Woolf.

CHEESE AND MILLET RISSOLES

1 onion
1 clove garlic
1 tablespoon olive oil
1 teaspoon cumin seeds
6 oz (175g) millet
3 oz (85g) wholewheat breadcrumbs
6 oz (175g) Cheddar cheese, grated
2 tablespoons toasted sunflower seeds
Sea salt and freshly ground black pepper
A little flour for coating
Oil for frying

Dice the onion and garlic and sauté in the olive oil with the cumin seeds until the onion is tender.

Dry roast the millet in a saucepan for a few minutes. Add water and cook, adding more water as necessary until the millet is very soft and moist.

Stir in the grated cheese, breadcrumbs, sunflower seeds, onion and garlic. Season with salt and pepper.

Lightly flour your hands and form the mixture into 12 balls. Heat a very little oil in a frying pan and fry the rissoles, turning as necessary until crispy and brown. Drain on kitchen paper.

Serve with mushroom or tomato sauce.

TURLU

A haricot bean stew, made luxuriantly creamy with lots of olive oil and potatoes and tasty with plenty of parsley and celery. It came to the Café through the Turkish International Night and is now a lunchtime standard.

8 oz (225g) haricot beans, soaked overnight
2 onions
2 small potatoes
1 carrot
1 head celery
6 tablespoons olive oil
6 tablespoons fresh parsley, chopped fine
Sea salt and freshly ground black pepper

Cook the haricot beans until nearly, but not quite, tender. Drain, reserving the cooking water.

Dice all the vegetables small. Sauté the onion in half the olive oil in a large saucepan until tender; add the rest of the vegetables and stir and cook for 15 minutes.

Add the haricot beans, half the parsley, the rest of the olive oil and ¾ pint (425ml) of haricot stock.

Put on the lid and simmer for 30-40 minutes, adding a little more stock as necessary until the potatoes are well fallen and the haricot beans very soft. Stir in the last of the parsley and season.

BEAN AND HAZELNUT RISOTTO

2 cloves garlic
6 oz (175g) green beans
3 oz (75g) hazelnuts
12 oz (350g) long-grain brown rice
1 tablespoon olive oil
2 teaspoons cumin seeds
1 pint (570ml) stock
1 glass medium-dry white wine
3 oz (75g) chickpeas, soaked overnight and cooked
1 tablespoon fresh parsley, chopped fine
Sea salt and freshly ground black pepper
2 tablespoons toasted sunflower seeds

Crush the garlic; chop the beans into 1-inch (2.5cm) lengths and roughly chop the hazelnuts, leaving some whole.

Put the garlic, hazelnuts, rice, olive oil and cumin seeds into a large pan and stir and roast over the heat for a few minutes. Pour in the stock and wine and bring to the boil. Put on the lid and reduce the heat.

After 25 minutes add the beans and chickpeas. Let the mixture steam for 15-20 minutes more until the rice is chewy and all of the liquid absorbed. Stir in the parsley and season with salt and pepper. Tip into a serving dish and scatter with the sunflower seeds.

Serve with herby white sauce or yogurt.

SAVOURY APRICOT RICE

12 oz (350g) long-grain brown rice
1 pint (570ml) water
½ teaspoon turmeric
2 bay leaves
1 large onion
1½ tablespoons olive oil
8 oz (225g) carrots
6 oz (175g) mushrooms
1 teaspoon thyme
Sea salt and freshly ground black pepper
2 oz (50g) dried apricots, soaked
1 oz (25g) currants
1 tablespoon fresh mint, chopped fine
A little stock

Put the rice, water, turmeric and bay leaves into a saucepan with a tightly fitting lid and cook until all of the water has been absorbed. The rice should be nearly, but not quite, tender. Drain and pour cold water through to keep the grains separate.

Preheat the oven to Gas Mark 5 (375°F/190°C).
Chop the onion and sauté in the olive oil until transparent. Slice the carrots into thin sticks and sauté with the onion until just tender.

Slice the mushrooms and add to the pan with the thyme and cook for 5 minutes more. Season and tip into a greased casserole dish.

Chop the apricots and mix into the rice with the currants and fresh mint. Layer over the carrot mixture and pour in a little stock. Bake for 30 minutes.

Serve with yogurt or yogurt sauce.

59

MUSHROOM AND CREAM TAGLIATELLE

12 oz (350g) button mushrooms
4 oz (110g) butter
½ pint (275ml) single cream
2 oz (55g) Parmesan, grated
¼ pint (140ml) yogurt
Sea salt and freshly ground black pepper
Freshly grated nutmeg
12 oz (350g) tagliatelle (green or wholewheat)

Bring a large pan of salted water to the boil.

Meanwhile, chop the mushrooms roughly and sauté in the butter for 5 minutes. Add the cream and grated Parmesan and when the Parmesan has melted stir in the yogurt. Keep warm but don't allow to boil. Season with salt, pepper and nutmeg.

Cook the tagliatelle. Drain and mix with the sauce on a large serving dish.

SPANISH TORTILLA

Not to be confused with Mexican tortillas, the Spanish tortilla is a vegetable omelette served hot or cold.

The recipe comes from an undaunted tortilla devotée who once spent a long July night in the hot café kitchen cooking dozens of tortillas for a Spanish menu.

2 onions
4-6 tablespoons olive oil
12 oz (350g) potatoes
3 cloves garlic
5 tomatoes
1 green pepper
1 teaspoon basil
½ teaspoon paprika
Sea salt and freshly ground black pepper
8 eggs
1 oz (25g) butter

Chop the onions and sauté in a little olive oil until soft. Set aside in a large bowl.

Slice the potatoes very thinly, dice the garlic and sauté together, adding more olive oil to the pan. When the potato is tender, add to the onion.

Quarter the tomatoes, chop the pepper and sauté in a little more oil. Add to the onion and potato. Stir in the basil and paprika and season with salt and pepper.

Beat the eggs, add to the vegetables and mix well. Melt the butter in the frying pan and pour in the mixture. Cook until the bottom is done then put under the grill to cook the top.

Slide onto a plate and cut into segments. (If your frying pan is small you may have to cook the mixture in 2 or 3 batches.)

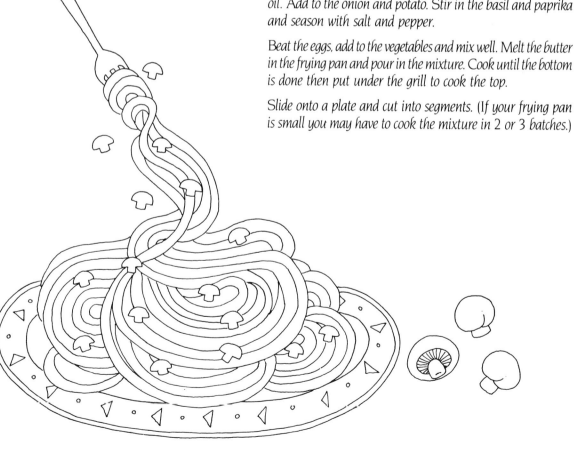

DOLMADIS (STUFFED VINE LEAVES)

The first Greek Night was rushed and chaotic as first International Nights often are. We were running late with the cooking and it seemed the final straw when we had to start folding a hundred or so vineleaves into tiny bundles. But it proved a surprisingly quick, rhythmic process and it was very satisfying when all the bundles were lying in rows under their tomato sauce, on time.

Vine leaves can be bought quite cheaply from many delicatessens and supermarkets.

8 oz (225g) long-grain brown rice
¼ teaspoon turmeric
1 onion
1 tomato
1 tablespoon olive oil
1 tablespoon currants
2 tablespoons pine nuts
1 teaspoon thyme
2 tablespoons fresh mint, chopped fine

Sea salt and freshly ground black pepper
½ teaspoon mace
26-30 vine leaves
Tomato sauce (see page 47)

Cook the rice with the turmeric, drain and run cold water through.

Dice the onion and tomato; heat the olive oil and sauté the onion until tender. Add the rice, currants, pine nuts, tomatoes, thyme and mint. Stir well and season with salt, pepper and mace.

Preheat the oven to Gas Mark 4 (350°F/180°C).

Rinse the vine leaves and drain.

To stuff, separate out a leaf and place it flat on the work surface. Spoon some of the mixture onto it, fold up the stem end then fold in the left and right corners and roll up to the top corner. After the first 2 or 3 vine leaves this becomes quick and easy. (If a leaf tears just wrap another round it.)
Arrange the bundles, fold downwards, in a lightly greased baking dish. Pour over the tomato sauce and bake for 30 minutes.

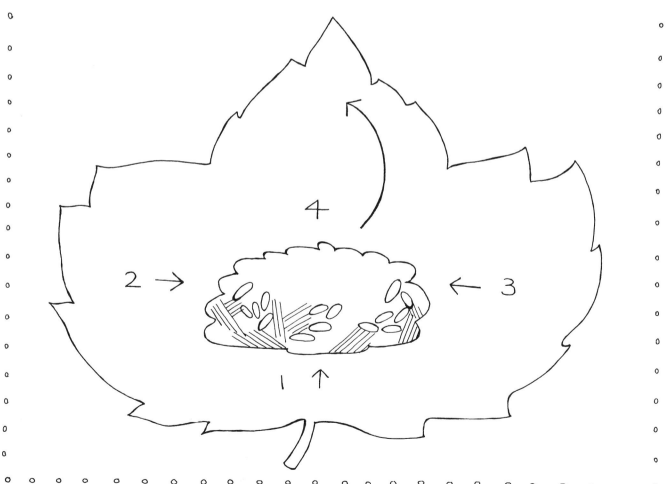

FELAFELS

Spicy, fried chickpea balls served in a warm pitta bread with plenty of salad.

8 oz (225g) chickpeas, soaked overnight
3 oz (75g) wholewheat breadcrumbs
2 cloves garlic
2 eggs, beaten
1 tablespoon fresh parsley, chopped fine
1 teaspoon cumin, ground
1 teaspoon coriander, ground
Sea salt
Oil for deep frying

Cook the chickpeas in boiling water for 15-20 minutes (they should be not quite tender).

Drain and grind in a food mill. Put them into a bowl and mix with the breadcrumbs, garlic, eggs, parsley, spices and salt. Leave to stand for half an hour.

Form into walnut-sized balls. Heat the oil until it begins to smoke and deep fry the balls until a rich golden-brown.

Drain on kitchen paper.

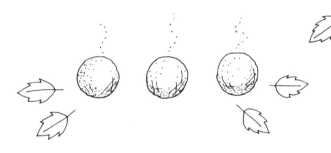

KASHA AND WALNUT-FILLED CABBAGE LEAVES

1 medium Dutch cabbage
6 oz (175g) buckwheat groats
2 tablespoons olive oil
1 onion
1 clove garlic
4 sticks celery
6 oz (175g) mushrooms
6 oz (175g) walnuts
1 teaspoon thyme
1 teaspoon marjoram
2 oz (50g) wholewheat breadcrumbs
2 tablespoons tahini
Dash of shoyu
Sea salt and freshly ground black pepper
Onion gravy (see page 46)
Apple sauce (see page 48)

to serve:

1 large lettuce
¼ cucumber
4 tomatoes
Fresh mint
Wholewheat pitta bread
Mayonnaise (see page 52)
Black olives
Vinaigrette (see page 51)

Shred the lettuce, dice the cucumber, cube the tomatoes, chop the mint and mix in a bowl.

Heat the pitta bread under a grill and cut open. Spread with mayonnaise and fill with 3 or 4 felafels and a generous spoonful of salad.

Top with olives and more mayonnaise or vinaigrette.

Slice the end off the cabbage. Cut deeply around the stalk and set the whole cabbage to cook in a large pan of water with a tight-fitting lid.

Check every now and again, and as each leaf lifts, remove from the cabbage and place in a bowl of cold water until you have 12.

Put the rest of the cabbage aside and keep the stock.

Roast the buckwheat in half the olive oil in a pan until it is nutty and toasted. Add water (2½ times as much as the buckwheat groats) and cook 35-40 minutes until chewy and tender.

Dice the onion and celery small, crush and chop the garlic, slice the mushrooms and roughly chop the walnuts. Sauté the onion, garlic, celery and herbs in the rest of the oil until tender. Add the mushrooms and nuts and sauté for a few minutes more. Mix in the buckwheat, breadcrumbs, tahini and shoyu. Season with salt and pepper. Add cabbage stock to bring to a moist consistency.

Place a generous tablespoonful of the mixture into each cabbage leaf and roll in the same way as for vineleaves (see page 61). Arrange fold-downwards in a greased baking dish. Use the cabbage stock to make an onion gravy and pour over the stuffed cabbage leaves. Cover, and bake at Gas Mark 4 (350°F/180°C) for 35-40 minutes.

Serve with apple sauce.

MOROCCAN COUS COUS

A Café friend who lived in Morocco for many years invited the Café collective to a meal at her house to demonstrate how couscous should be prepared and served. Her kitchen was filled with a long, extended table, on which were two huge plates piled high with the soft grain and topped with a luscious vegetable sauce. We all sat round the table as she proceeded to show us the technique, rolling a little couscous and sauce into a ball in her hand and tossing it into her mouth. And so began a long and boisterous evening.

We haven't yet dared introduce such an authentic note to the Café, but we do encourage you to do so at home.

VEGETABLE SAUCE

1 onion
2 cloves garlic
1 small green chilli
1 lb (450g) tomatoes
2 courgettes
4 medium potatoes
1 lb (450g) pumpkin
8 oz (225g) carrots
½ bunch fresh coriander
2 tablespoons soya oil
1 teaspoon ground coriander
1 teaspoon turmeric
1 teaspoon ground cumin
1 teaspoon thyme
Sea salt and freshly ground black pepper

Slice the onion and dice the garlic; halve the chilli, remove the seeds and chop fine. Quarter the tomatoes, slice the courgettes, chop the potatoes and pumpkin into chunks, slice the carrots into sticks and roughly chop the fresh coriander.

Heat the oil in a large saucepan and sauté the onion and garlic until the onion is soft. Add the spices, green chilli and potato and sauté for a further 5 minutes. Add the tomatoes and stir and cook a little more.

Add all the other ingredients except for the coriander leaves and pour in ½ pint (275ml) stock or water. Bring to the boil and simmer for 30 minutes until everything is tender. Season with salt and pepper.

Stir in the coriander leaves during the last few minutes of cooking.

THE COUS COUS

12 oz (350g) couscous
12 fl oz (350ml) warm water containing a little sea salt
1 tablespoon olive oil or butter

Put the couscous in a bowl and pour ¾ of the salted water over it.

Stir and then leave to stand for 10 minutes. Break up with a fork to get rid of any lumps. Add the remaining water and repeat the process. Stir in the butter or olive oil.

Put in a colander, cover with a lid or tea towel and steam on the pot of cooking vegetables for 20-30 minutes.

VEGETABLE CHOP SUEY

The preparation of this dish can make quite a welcome change from the usual Café kitchen routine of fast, hectic chopping and cooking, for an important point of the recipe is that the vegetables should be attractively sliced into evenly shaped pieces. So it requires an hour of careful, thoughtful chopping. The order in which the vegetables are put into the pot is also very important so that everything becomes just tender at the same time.

**1 inch (2.5cm) fresh ginger
2 cloves garlic
1 large leek
½ head celery
8 oz (225g) carrots
1 small spring cabbage
1 small cauliflower
6 oz (175g) mushrooms
1 tablespoon olive oil
1 teaspoon cumin seeds
Stock
6 oz (175g) beansprouts
1 tablespoon arrowroot
1-2 tablespoons tamari
Freshly ground black pepper**

Dice the ginger and garlic fine. Slice the leeks into rings, the celery into thin lengths and the carrots into diagonal rings. Shred the cabbage and chop the cauliflower into florets. Halve any large mushrooms and leave the rest whole.

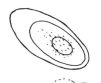

Heat the oil in a large saucepan and sauté the ginger, garlic, cumin seed, leek, carrot, celery and cauliflower. Stir well to coat with oil. Add stock to reach the top of the vegetables, bring to the boil and simmer.

After 5 minutes add the spring cabbage. When everything is turning tender add the mushrooms and two minutes later the bean sprouts. Leave these on top to cook in the steam.

Mix the arrowroot to a paste with cold water and 1 tablespoon tamari and stir into the chop suey. Taste and adjust the seasoning with more tamari or pepper. If the sauce is too thick add more stock, if too thin, more arrowroot.

Serve immediately, with rice or noodles.

AUBERGINE JAMAICA

The Café cooks learn a great deal when planning and cooking for the International Nights. Occasionally new dishes are concocted as a result of blending the cooking traditions of two or more countries. This dish was first made one lunchtime by a cook inspired by both the Caribbean and Sri Lankan nights.

It is a delicious mixture of potatoes and aubergines baked in coconut cream.

1 large aubergine
Sea salt
8 oz (225g) potatoes
½ head celery
8 oz (225g) mushrooms
1 tablespoon olive oil

sauce:

6 oz (175g) creamed coconut
2 green chillies
½ teaspoon celery seeds
1½ tablespoons tahini
¼ teaspoon cayenne pepper
15 curry leaves, chopped
1 tablespoon sesame seeds

Preheat the oven to Gas Mark 4 (350°F/180°C).

Slice the aubergine thinly, sprinkle with salt and leave for 30 minutes. This draws out any bitterness. Rinse and squeeze dry.

Bake on a baking tray for 30 minutes.

Meanwhile, cook the potatoes until tender and drain, reserving the stock. When cool enough to handle, slice the potatoes thinly. Dice the celery, slice the mushrooms and sauté both in the olive oil.

To make the sauce dissolve the creamed coconut in ½ pint (275ml) of the potato stock. Halve the chillies, carefully remove the seeds, dice and stir into the sauce with celery seeds, tahini, cayenne and curry leaves. Simmer for a few minutes to blend the flavours but do not allow to boil.

Now layer everything in a greased casserole, starting with half the potatoes, then the aubergines, then half the coconut sauce, the rest of the potatoes, the mushrooms and celery, and finally the rest of the coconut sauce. Sprinkle the top with sesame seeds.

Cover and bake for 45 minutes, taking the lid off for the last 10 minutes.

CHILLI BEANS

1 lb (450g) red kidney beans, soaked overnight
2 small onions
2 cloves garlic
1 green pepper
2 tablespoons olive oil
1 lb (450g) tomatoes
1 teaspoon oregano
2 teaspoons ground cumin
1-2 teaspoons chilli powder
2 tablespoons fresh coriander, chopped fine

Drain the soaked beans and cook in fresh water until tender. Drain. Dice the onion, garlic and green pepper and sauté in the olive oil in a large pan until tender. Roughly chop the tomatoes and add to the pan with the oregano. Cook and stir until everything is very soft. Add enough water to make a thick sauce. Stir in the beans and cumin powder, and carefully add chilli powder to taste. Simmer to blend the flavours for 15 minutes or so.

Serve with rice. Garnish with coriander leaves and, if you like, yogurt.

LEEK AND POTATO BAKE

There is an urban farm in Leeds which grows organic vegetables of a very high quality and as each type is harvested some are brought to the Café. These deliveries often arrive unexpectedly and in large enough amounts to pose problems for the cooks. The sudden need to deal with boxes of potatoes and leeks led to this Leek and Potato Bake recipe.

These two vegetables combine deliciously, and here they are simply sliced and baked in butter together.

1 lb (450g) potatoes
1 lb (450g) leeks
3 oz (75g) Cheddar cheese, grated
Sea salt and freshly ground black pepper
A little butter

Preheat the oven to Gas Mark 7 (425°F/220°C).

Scrub the potatoes and slice as thinly as possible. Leave to soak in a bowl of cold water for 15 minutes or so.

Meanwhile, wash the leeks thoroughly (see page 24) and slice thinly. Lightly oil a casserole dish and layer the vegetables in it, starting and finishing with a potato layer. Put a sprinkling of cheese in the middle and season with black pepper and a little salt. Top with the rest of the cheese and a few butter dots.

Bake for 1 hour until bubbling and brown.

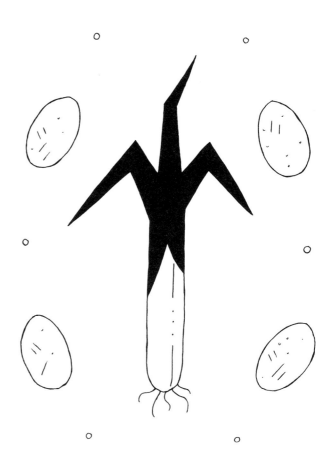

■　□　■　□　■　□　■　□　■

SPINACH LASAGNE

2 tablespoons olive oil
Sea salt and freshly ground black pepper
6 oz (175g) wholewheat lasagne
5 oz (150g) brown lentils
1 large onion
4 sticks celery
2 cloves garlic
6 oz (175g) mushrooms
4 oz (110g) Edam cheese, grated
1 tablespoon tamari
2 oz (50g) wholewheat breadcrumbs
2 teaspoons oregano
1 egg
1 lb (450g) spinach
½ pint (275ml) cheese sauce (see page 44)

Preheat the oven to Gas Mark 5 (375°F/190°C).

Bring a large pan of water, with a little oil and salt, to the boil. Put in the lasagne carefully and cook until just barely soft (al dente). Drain and put aside in a large bowl of cold water.

At the same time cook the brown lentils until tender and drain. Chop the onions and celery finely, crush the garlic and slice the mushrooms. Sauté in the olive oil until tender; then add the cooked lentils, half the Edam, the tamari, breadcrumbs, oregano and beaten egg. Stir well and season with salt and pepper.

Shred the spinach and steam.

Now the lasagne can be assembled. Grease a deep oven dish and line with some lasagne sheets. Pour the lentil and mushroom mixture over this and top with another layer of lasagne. Cover with the rest of the Edam, and then the spinach. Top with another layer of lasagne and pour the cheese sauce over this. Bake for 35 minutes until golden-brown.

Serve with a large green salad.

POTATO AND SPINACH LAYER BAKE

**1 lb (450g) potatoes
1 medium onion
1 tablespoon soya oil
¼ teaspoon paprika
1 teaspoon ground cumin
¼ teaspoon nutmeg
1 lb (450g) spinach
3 oz (75g) Cheddar cheese, grated
1 tablespoon black poppyseeds
2 eggs
¼ pint (150ml) milk
Sea salt and freshly ground black pepper**

Preheat the oven to Gas Mark 6 (400°F/200°C).

Scrub the potatoes and boil until tender. Chop the onion finely and sauté in the soya oil in a large pan until transparent. Add the paprika, cumin and nutmeg and sauté for a few minutes longer.

Shred the spinach, add to the onion and cook until just wilting and soft. Cut the potatoes into slices and place a layer in an oiled baking dish.

Sprinkle with half the grated cheese and half the poppyseeds. Place the onion and spinach on top of this, and then another layer of potato slices. Sprinkle with the remaining cheese and poppyseeds. Beat the eggs with the milk and a little salt and pepper and pour over.

Bake for 40-45 minutes until a knife poked in comes out clean.

BROCCOLI AND MILLET BAKED IN YOGURT

Just before 12 o'clock the day's menu is written up on a blackboard near the counter. Names for the various dishes are thought up while tidying the kitchen in readiness for serving, and then shouted out to the person chalking the menu. And though an evocative, exciting title is sought, the imagination often fails under the stress of sweeping the floor, adding a little more of something to the soup, wondering where the milk is and remembering that the urn hasn't been put on yet. So this excellent dish comes to you as merely Broccoli and Millet Baked in Yogurt.

**8 oz (225g) millet
8 oz (225g) broccoli
1 onion
1 large leek
1 tablespoon oil
1 egg
½ pint (275ml) yogurt
4 oz (110g) Cheddar cheese, grated
1 teaspoon basil
½ teaspoon dill seeds (optional)
Sea salt and freshly ground black pepper
1 tablespoon sesame seeds**

Dry-roast the millet in a pan, stirring until it is just beginning to brown and smell toasted. Add water and cook until soft and fluffy.

Chop the broccoli florets, stalks and leaves and steam until tender.

Chop the onion and leek fairly small and sauté in the oil. Then mix all these with the millet in a large bowl.

Beat the egg with half the yogurt, stir in the cheese and pour into the millet mixture. Mix well, stir in the basil and dill seed and season with salt and pepper.

Pile into a well-oiled casserole dish. Mix the rest of the yogurt with the rest of the cheese and pour over the top. Scatter with sesame seeds and bake covered at Gas Mark 5 (375°F/190°C) for 30 minutes.

NUT ROAST

Unfortunately the nut roast has gained a reputation as a vegetarian apology for meat. Such an idea can only have come from those who have never tried it, for a nut roast is exquisite and by no means a substitute for anything else. It has become traditional fare at the café over Christmas.

HAZELNUT AND MUSHROOM ROAST

4 oz (110g) bulgur (cracked wheat)
1 large onion
½ head celery
2 tablespoons soya oil
1 teaspoon marjoram
4 oz (110g) mushrooms
3 oz (75g) mixed nuts, such as walnuts, cashews, brazils
4 oz (110g) hazelnuts
2 oz (50g) wholewheat breadcrumbs
1 teaspoon sage
1 bay leaf
1 tablespoon fresh parsley, chopped fine
1 tablespoon tamari or shoyu
Sea salt and freshly ground black pepper

Preheat the oven to Gas Mark 4 (350°F/180°C).

Place the bulgur into a bowl, pour boiling water over to cover, and leave for 30 minutes or so until the water has been absorbed.

Meanwhile, dice the onion and celery finely and sauté in the oil with the marjoram until nearly tender. Slice the mushrooms, add to the pan and cook for 5 minutes or so.

Grind the nuts, leaving a few roughly chopped and whole. Now mix the bulgur, breadcrumbs, onion and mushroom mixture, ground nuts, herbs and tamari together in a large bowl. Beat the egg and stir in. Season with salt and pepper. It should have a sticky, wet consistency, so add a little stock if necessary. Tip into a large, well-oiled loaf tin and bake for 45 minutes.

Serve with a sauce, such as watercress sauce.
Vegan:
Substitute 2 tablespoons olive oil for the egg.

BRAZIL NUT AND SPRING CABBAGE ROAST

1 onion
3 sticks celery
2 tablespoons corn oil
8 oz (225g) spring cabbage
8 oz (225g) brazil nuts
4 oz (110g) mixed nuts
8 oz (225g) wholewheat breadcrumbs
1 teaspoon basil
1 teaspoon thyme
1 egg
Sea salt and freshly ground black pepper
1 tablespoon shoyu

Preheat the oven to Gas Mark 4 (350°F/180°C).

Dice the onion and celery small and sauté in the corn oil with the herbs until tender. Shred the spring cabbage finely and steam.

Grind the nuts, leaving a few roughly chopped and whole. Mix the nuts, vegetables, breadcrumbs and herbs in a large bowl. Stir in the beaten egg and enough cabbage stock to bring to a sticky, wet consistency. Season with salt and pepper and shoyu. Tip into a large, well-oiled bread tin and bake for 45 minutes.

Serve with a white sauce, such as herby sauce.
Vegan:
Substitute 5 oz (150ml) tofu and ¼ pint (150ml) soya milk for the egg.

CAULIFLOWER AND MUSHROOM LOAF

2 medium cauliflowers
1 medium onion
1 tablespoon olive oil
8 oz (225g) mushrooms
3 oz (75g) wholewheat breadcrumbs
1 egg
2 tablespoons fresh parsley, chopped fine
Sea salt and freshly ground black pepper
Freshly grated nutmeg
1 dessertspoon shoyu
2 oz (50g) Cheddar cheese grated

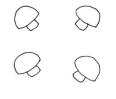

Preheat the oven to Gas Mark 4 (350°F/180°C).

Chop the cauliflower roughly, discarding any tough, outer leaves and steam until tender, then mash. Dice the onion and sauté in the heated olive oil until transparent. Slice the mushrooms, add to the pan and sauté a few minutes longer. Stir into the mashed cauliflower. Add three-quarters of the breadcrumbs, the beaten egg and parsley and mix well. Season with salt, pepper, nutmeg and shoyu.

Tip into a large, greased loaf tin and top with the remaining breadcrumbs and cheese.

Bake for 1 hour.

BAKED RED CABBAGE

1 medium red cabbage
3 cooking apples
2 large onions
2 tablespoons cider vinegar
2 teaspoons aniseed
1 tablespoon clear honey
½ pint (275ml) stock
Sea salt and freshly ground black pepper

Preheat the oven to Gas Mark 2 (300°F/150°C).

Shred the cabbage and dice the apples and onions. Mix everything together and tip into a large well-oiled casserole dish with a lid.

Bake slowly for up to 3 hours.

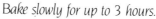

70

CURRIES

Serve 2 or more of the following curries, with rice or chapattis and one or two raitas.

COURGETTE CURRY

2½ lb (1125g) courgettes
2 inches (5cm) ginger
3 tablespoons ghee
1 teaspoon salt
4 teaspoons turmeric
2 tablespoons ground coriander
1 teaspoon cayenne
½ pint (275ml) yogurt

Cut the courgettes into quarters lengthways and then into 2-inch (5cm) lengths. Peel and dice the ginger and fry in the ghee with the salt and turmeric for 1 minute. Add the courgettes and fry until tender and a bit fallen.

Take from the heat. Mix the coriander and cayenne into the yogurt and stir into the courgettes. Reheat very gently without boiling and serve.

This curry goes particularly well with couscous (see page 63) for method of cooking).

SPINACH AND MUSHROOM CURRY

Replace the courgettes with 2 lb (900g) spinach and 1 lb (450g) mushrooms.

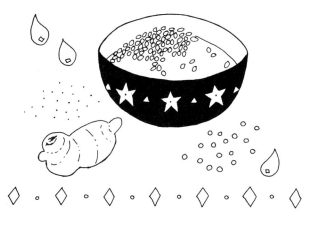

DAL

Dal making took on spectacular proportions when the Café catered for an out-of-doors weekend event one year. We used a sack of lentils and a sack of onions and measured spices into the pan by the tablespoon. It is a rich, orangy-yellow dish, and was comforting during the periods of rain over the weekend and yet spicily appropriate in the hot, sunny patches as well.

12 oz (350g) red lentils, soaked for at least an hour
2 onions
2 cloves garlic
1 inch (2.5cm) fresh ginger
3 tablespoons ghee
½ teaspoon chilli powder
2 teaspoons turmeric
2 teaspoons poppyseeds
2 teaspoons coriander seeds
2 teaspoons cumin seeds
4 black peppercorns
8 cloves
2-inch (5cm) cinnamon stick
1 teaspoon sea salt

Drain the lentils and set to cook in fresh water. Peel and dice the onions, garlic and ginger and sauté in the ghee until the onions are golden.

Meanwhile, grind the chilli powder, turmeric, poppyseeds, coriander seeds, cumin seeds, peppercorns, cloves, cinnamon stick and sea salt. Add to the onions and cook for a few minutes.

Stir into the lentils. Reduce by further cooking or add water to bring to the desired consistency.

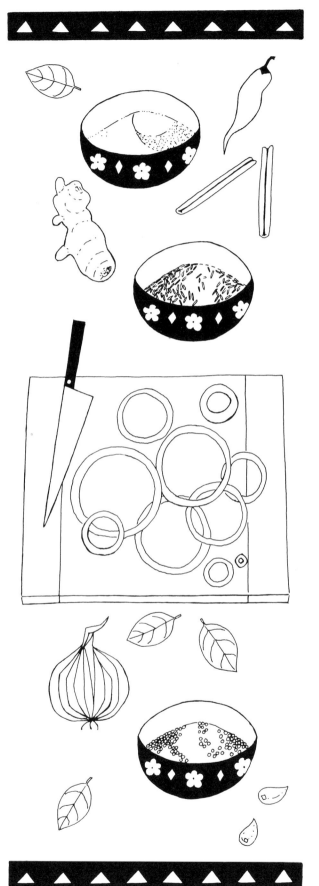

VEGETABLE CURRY

sauce:

2 onions
4 cloves garlic
4 tablespoons ghee
2 green peppers
8 oz (225g) mushrooms
2 teaspoons coriander seeds
1 teaspoon cayenne pepper
½ teaspoon cinnamon
4 broken cardamoms
2 teaspoons turmeric
2 teaspoons fenugreek
2 teaspoons ground cumin
2 teaspoons black mustard seed
1 teaspoon sea salt
4 tablespoons desiccated coconut
1 tablespoon tomato purée
Juice of a lemon
½ pint (275ml) yogurt
½ pint (275ml) stock
2 oz (50g) cashews

vegetables:

2 potatoes
2 carrots
2 parsnips
Small spring cabbage, or 8 oz (225g) spinach
2 courgettes
4 oz (110g) green beans
4 tomatoes

Chop the onions and garlic and fry in the ghee until the onion is soft. Dice the green pepper, slice the mushrooms, add to the pan and fry for 3 or 4 minutes. Stir in the spices, seeds and salt and fry for 4 minutes more. Add 1 or 2 tablespoons of cold water, turning the heat up so everything sizzles furiously. Repeat, to make a fairly thick sauce. Take off the heat and stir in the desiccated coconut, tomato purée, lemon juice, yogurt, stock and cashews. Return to the heat and simmer very gently.

Chop the potatoes, carrots and parsnips into fairly small slices and boil until just tender. Shred the spring cabbage, slice the courgettes and beans, then steam. Chop the tomatoes into quarters. Add all of this to the sauce and simmer for 10 minutes or so to heat through and blend the flavours.

GREEN BANANA CURRY

A mild, fruity curry that makes a good accompaniment to a hot one.

4 green bananas
1 teaspoon sea salt
1 teaspoon turmeric
2 tablespoons ghee
6 oz (175g) coconut cream
2 green chillies
1 onion
½ teaspoon fenugreek seeds
10 curry leaves
1 inch (2.5cm) cinnamon

Peel the bananas, cut into halves crossways and then into quarters lengthways. Rub in the salt and turmeric. Heat the ghee in a frying pan and sauté the banana pieces until golden-brown all over.

Melt the coconut cream in a pan with 1 pint (570ml) water. Halve the chillies, de-seed and dice; chop the onion fine. Add both to the pan with the fenugreek seeds, curry leaves and cinnamon and cook until the onion is soft. Add the bananas, stir well and cook for a few minutes longer to blend the flavours.

POTATO CURRY

2 inches (5 cm) fresh ginger
4 cloves garlic
2 onions
1 green pepper
6 oz (175g) mushrooms
3 tablespoons ghee
1 teaspoon salt
1 teaspoon mace
1½ teaspoons ground coriander
1½ teaspoons ground cumin
¼ teaspoon chilli powder
2 teaspoons turmeric
1 lb (450g) potatoes

Peel the ginger and garlic and dice finely. Slice the onions and pepper; halve any very large mushrooms and leave the rest whole.

Heat the ghee in a heavy based pan and sauté the onion, garlic and ginger until the onion is transparent. Stir in the salt and all the spices and cook for 2-3 minutes. Then add the pepper and mushrooms and stir and cook for 5 minutes more.

Chop the potatoes into 1 inch (2.5 cm) pieces, add to the pan and stir and cook for a further 2 minutes. Then pour in enough water to just cover the potatoes and cook on a medium heat until everything is tender.

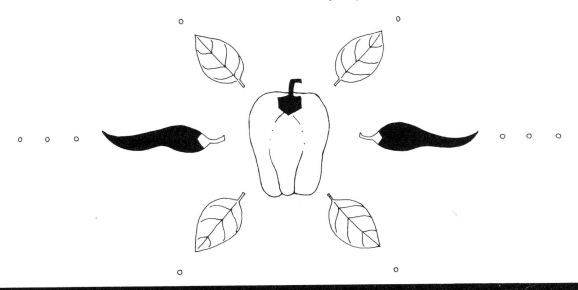

RAITAS

*A raita brings the cooling, tart taste of yogurt to a curry meal.
Serve in a large bowl with a deep spoon so that people can help
themselves.*

MANGO RAITA

*There is a treat in store for those making this raita — mango
stones can never be cut quite clean of mango flesh so must be
left orange and juicy to chew on.*

1 ripe mango
1 green chilli
1 pint (570ml) yogurt
1 teaspoon ground cumin
¼ teaspoon sea salt

Peel the mango, cut the flesh from the stone and chop roughly.
Tip into a bowl with as much juice as you can recover from the
chopping board. Halve the chilli, de-seed carefully and dice; add
to the bowl. Beat in the yogurt, ground cumin and a little salt.

FENNEL RAITA

1 small fennel bulb
1 tablespoon fresh coriander leaves, chopped
1 pint (570ml) yogurt
½ teaspoon ground coriander
¼ teaspoon sea salt
Pinch paprika

Slice the fennel finely and put into a serving bowl with the
chopped coriander leaves. Beat in the yogurt, ground coriander
and salt.

Garnish with a few extra coriander leaves and a sprinkle of
paprika.

BANANA RAITA

Substitute one large banana, sliced fine, for the mango.

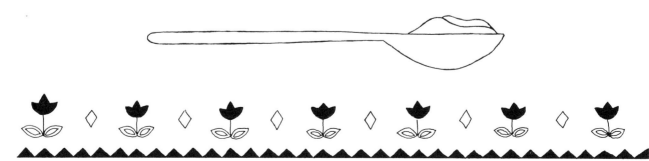

Every Wednesday evening, the Café workers have a long meeting up in the office to talk about the Café's finances, future and the coming week. There is a meal-break half way through and everyone comes downstairs to the kitchen to make something quickly to eat. Usually a few vegetables are sliced, thrown into a sizzling wok in a mixture of colours, shapes and textures, and stirred and sautéed until tender, yet still a little crisp. This is shared onto plates with a grain and sometimes a sauce and taken into one of the dining rooms. The curtains are drawn on the dark streets outside, a few chairs are taken down from the tables (where they were put for afternoon's sweeping) and everyone eats.

STIR-FRIED VEGETABLES

Stir-fried vegetables make a beautifully simple dish. It is infinitely adaptable and the following list of ingredients is intended only as a guideline. You can use just one kind of vegetable, three, four or many, and they can be highly seasoned or hardly at all. Ginger and tamari bring a Chinese flavour that is particularly appropriate in a stir-fry, and lemon juice, garlic, nuts, seeds or herbs add variety. But the wok, a large, rounded Chinese pan, is the essential part. It has a large surface area and so can cook a great number of vegetables evenly and all at once. Choose a selection from the following vegetables and seasonings.

Carrots, sliced into thin diagonals.
Turnips, chopped into matchsticks
Green beans, sliced into 2 inch (5 cm) lengths
Red or green peppers, sliced into narrow strips
Cauliflower or broccoli, chopped into florets
Mushrooms, sliced thinly, or if small, left whole
Red or white, or spring cabbage, shredded finely
Bean shoots
Onions, sliced into circles
Ginger and garlic, peeled and diced
Parsley, chives or spring onions, chopped fine
Squeeze of lemon juice
Tamari
Hazelnuts, cashews, sesame seeds or sunflower seeds, toasted
Stock
Olive oil

Heat a tablespoon or so of olive oil in a wok. If you are using several kinds of vegetables, add in stages, beginning with those which take longest to cook, such as carrots and turnips, then, after a few minutes, slightly softer vegetables such as green beans, peppers, cauliflower and broccoli, then mushrooms and finally beanshoots and leafy vegetables, which need only wilt.

Onion, garlic and ginger should be added at the start so their flavours permeate throughout the cooking time.

Keep the heat fairly high and stir constantly so that all the vegetables reach the sides of the pan.

You will probably need to pour in a little stock or water — just enough to add moisture and prevent sticking, but not so much as to leave excess liquid.

Stir in tamari, or lemon juice towards the end of cooking to taste.

Nuts, seeds or herbs can also be stirred in towards the end or scattered on top as a garnish.

Serve on rice, buckwheat, bulgur or noodles, accompanied perhaps with a sauce such as tamari and ginger sauce (page 46) or yogurt and gomasio (page 54).

RICE

Brown rice is so versatile as an accompaniment to vegetables, curries and stews and as an ingredient in main meals and salads. To cook, place one part of rice with two parts of cold water in a pan, put on a tight-fitting lid and bring to the boil. Then turn the heat down and simmer for 45 minutes. The water should all be absorbed. Stir with a fork and serve.

1½ cups of uncooked rice is sufficient for 4-6 people.

Variations:

Many things can be added to rice during cooking to vary its flavour and appearance. The following quantities refer to 1½ cups of uncooked rice.

SEEDS AND NUTS

1 or 2 tablespoons sunflower seeds, or sesame seeds, roughly chopped hazelnuts, almonds, walnuts or cashews can be cooked with the rice. Sauté the seed or nut with the rice in a little olive oil first, then add the water and proceed as usual.

HERBED RICE

1 teaspoon basil, thyme, dill or marjoram can be added to the rice during cooking. Or stir 2 tablespoons finely chopped fresh parsley and a squeeze of lemon juice into the rice after it is cooked.

SAVOURY RICE

2 bay leaves
3 crushed cardamom pods
2 teaspoons caraway seeds
1 dessertspoon olive oil or ghee

Sauté the rice with the bay leaves, cardamom pods, and caraway seeds in the oil for a few minutes, then add the water and cook as usual.

GOLDEN RICE

Add 1 teaspoon turmeric to the rice and cook as usual.

CURRANT RICE

1 tablespoon currants
1 inch (2.5cm) stick of cinnamon, crushed
3 cloves
½ teaspoon turmeric

Add everything to the rice and cook as usual.

RICE WITH GARLIC AND GINGER

1 onion
2 cloves garlic
1 inch (2.5 cm) piece of ginger
1 tablespoon olive oil or ghee

Peel and finely dice the onion, garlic and ginger and sauté in the oil until the onion is soft. Add the rice, sauté for a minute longer, then add the water and cook as usual.

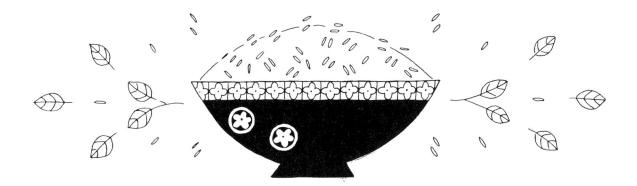

PANCAKES

Occasionally, one of us decides to make a few pancakes for our breakfast. Eaten with maple syrup, lemon juice or just butter they are always a treat. They are sometimes made on a grander scale for the customers, at lunchtime or in the evening, as a main meal or dessert.

Frying for large numbers can be hot, steamy work, but it is enjoyable to pile a plate higher and higher with golden, warm-smelling pancakes. They are then filled with something sweet or savoury, rolled, sauced and heated through in the oven, and make a very popular dish, so popular that the Café is thinking of dedicating a night a week to them.

Pancake making can seem a difficult art but really it is easy. Always leave the batter to stand for at least 30 minutes, and use a shallow frying pan quite hot with only a very little oil and all your pancakes will be perfect.

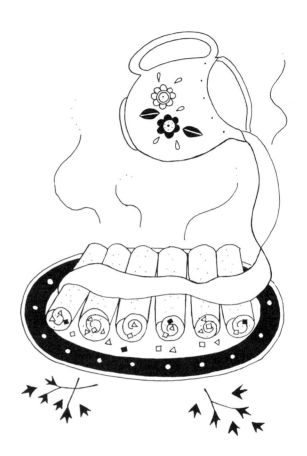

PANCAKE BATTER
For 12 pancakes

6 oz (175g) wholewheat flour
Pinch of sea salt
1 egg and an extra yolk
¾ pint (425ml) milk
Oil for frying

Sieve the flour into a bowl, add the salt and make a well in the centre. Beat the egg, egg yolk and half the milk separately and pour into the well. Beat thoroughly, pour in the remaining milk and beat again until smooth. Leave to stand for 30 minutes.

Now heat a little oil in a shallow frying pan, drain off any excess oil and spoon in just enough batter to cover the bottom of the pan when tipped to spread the mixture (about 3 tablespoons per pancake). Cook until set, then turn and cook the other side. Add a little extra oil to the pan after every 4 pancakes or so and drain off any excess as before.

PANCAKE FILLINGS:

LEEK FILLING

1¾ lb (800g) leeks
¾ pint (425ml) white sauce (see page 44)
Freshly grated nutmeg
Sea salt and freshly ground black pepper
3 oz (75g) Cheddar cheese, grated

Wash the leeks well (see page 24), slice into 1-inch (2.5 cm) lengths and steam until tender.

Mix with half the white sauce and season with nutmeg, salt and pepper. Spoon 1-2 tablespoons into each pancake, roll and arrange in a buttered baking dish. Melt the cheese in the rest of the sauce, pour over the pancakes and heat through in a hot oven 5-10 minutes.

SPINACH FILLING

Follow the Leek Filling recipe substituting 1¾ lb (800g) spinach for the leeks.

MUSHROOM AND SOUR CREAM FILLING

1 onion
2 garlic cloves
1 lb (450g) mushrooms
1½ tablespoons butter
1 teaspoon thyme
6 tablespoons sour cream
Sea salt and freshly ground black pepper

Slice the onion and chop the garlic. Slice 6 mushrooms neatly and keep separate. Chop the rest roughly, leaving any small ones whole.

Sauté the reserved mushroom slices in a little of the butter for a few seconds, then remove and put to one side. Put the rest of the butter in the pan and sauté the onions and garlic until turning golden. Add the mushrooms and thyme and cook for a few minutes longer.

Stir in half the sour cream. Put 1-2 tablespoons of filling into each pancake, roll and arrange in a buttered baking tray. Spoon over the remaining sour cream and garnish with sautéed mushroom slices.

Heat through in a hot oven for 5-10 minutes.

SUMMER VEGETABLE FILLING

12 oz (350g) courgettes
6 oz (175g) small, new carrots
8 oz (225g) button mushrooms
2 onions
1 bunch watercress
1 tablespoon butter
Juice of ½ a lemon
¾ pint (425ml) white sauce (page 44)
Freshly grated nutmeg
Sea salt and freshly ground black pepper
3 oz (75g) Cheddar cheese, grated

Dice the courgettes and carrots small and steam until tender. Slice the mushrooms and onions thinly and roughly chop the watercress.

Sauté the onions in the butter until soft, then add the mushrooms and sauté for 3-5 minutes more.

Stir in the lemon juice, watercress, courgettes and carrots, and a quarter of the white sauce. Season with salt and pepper and plenty of nutmeg. Spoon 1-2 tablespoons of the mixture into each pancake, roll and arrange in a buttered baking dish. Melt the grated cheese in the rest of the sauce, pour over the pancakes and heat through in a hot oven for 5-10 minutes.

RATATOUILLE FILLING

1 aubergine
Sea salt and freshly ground black pepper
2 garlic cloves
1 onion
2 red peppers
4 oz (110g) mushrooms
2 carrots
2 courgettes
3 tomatoes
2 tablespoons olive oil
1 tablespoon fresh parsley, chopped fine
1 teaspoon marjoram
¼ pint (150ml) tomato sauce (see page 47)

Slice the aubergine into thin semi-circles, arrange across a tray, sprinkle with salt and leave for half an hour (this draws out any bitterness). At the end of this time rinse and squeeze dry.

Meanwhile, chop the garlic fine and slice the onion, red peppers and mushrooms. Dice the carrots, courgettes and tomatoes. Heat the oil in a large saucepan and sauté the onion, garlic and aubergine. After 5-10 minutes add the rest of the ingredients, except the tomato sauce. Stir well and simmer 20-30 minutes until everything is very tender.

Spoon 1-2 tablespoons into each pancake, roll and arrange in a buttered baking tray. Pour the tomato sauce over the pancakes and heat through in a hot oven for 5-10 minutes.

APPLE FILLING

2½ lb (125g) Bramley apples
2-3 tablespoons water
4 cloves
2 oz (50g) raw cane sugar, or to taste
¼ pint (150ml) single cream
¼ teaspoon cinnamon

Peel, core and cube the apples. Stew with the water, cloves and sugar until just tender. Spoon 1-2 tablespoons into each pancake, roll and arrange in a buttered baking dish. Pour the single cream over the pancakes and sprinkle with the cinnamon.

Heat through in a hot oven for 5 minutes or so.

APRICOT FILLING

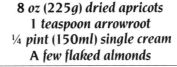

8 oz (225g) dried apricots
1 teaspoon arrowroot
¼ pint (150ml) single cream
A few flaked almonds

Cook the apricots in a little water until tender, drain and reserve the liquid. Make up to ¼ pint (150ml) with water, return to the pan and bring to the boil. Mix the arrowroot in a little water and add to the liquid to make a syrup.

Pour over the apricots. Spoon 1 tablespoon of the mixture into each pancake, roll and arrange in a buttered baking dish. Pour over the cream and scatter with the flaked almonds.

Heat through in a hot oven for 5 minutes.

STRAWBERRY FILLING

1 lb (450g) strawberries
2 tablespoons dry white wine
2 teaspoons raw cane sugar, or to taste
¼ pint (150ml) whipping cream or sour cream

Tail the strawberries and halve or quarter, depending on size. Soak in the wine and sugar and leave aside while making the pancakes.

When ready for the filling, whip all but 2 tablespoons of the cream. Stir the strawberries into the whipped cream, reserving their juice.

Spoon 1-2 tablespoons of the strawberries into each pancake, roll and arrange in a buttered baking dish. Pour over the remaining cream and strawberry syrup.

Heat through in a hot oven for 5 minutes.

MEXICAN PANCAKES

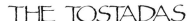

Tostadas and tacos are types of tortillas — mexican corn pancakes.
A tostada is made up of lightly fried tortillas stacked with cheesy,
beany and vegetable fillings between the layers. A taco is a crisp
tortilla folded into a pocket for filling. Both are widely available
from supermarkets and delicatessans.

THE TOSTADAS

12 tortillas
4 oz (110g) Cheddar cheese, grated
Corn oil for frying

Heat a little corn oil in a frying pan on high heat. Fry each tortilla
on both sides until crisp, piling on a plate as each is done.

Cover half the tortillas with the re-fried bean mixture. Place
another tortilla on top of each and cover with the vegetable
mixture.

Top with a little grated cheese and put into a medium oven for
10 minutes or so — just long enough to melt the cheese and
heat everything through.

BEAN TACOS

1 lettuce
3 tomatoes
1 avocado
6 taco shells
Re-fried Bean Filling (see this page)
¼ pint (150ml) sour cream

Shred the lettuce, dice the tomatoes and peel and slice the avocado.

Heat the taco shells a little under the grill or in the oven and
fill each with a generous spoonful of the bean mixture, lettuce,
tomato, avocado slices and a dollop of sour cream.

THE FILLINGS

RE-FRIED BEAN FILLING

4 oz (110g) pinto beans, soaked overnight
3 oz (75g) red kidney beans, soaked overnight
2 onions
½ green pepper
2 cloves garlic
2 tablespoons olive oil
2 teaspoons ground coriander
½ teaspoon ground mustard
2 teaspoons ground cumin
½ teaspoon paprika
Dash of shoyu
Sea salt and freshly ground black pepper

Cook the two types of bean separately until they are soft. Drain,
combine and mash well. Dice the onions, green pepper and garlic
and sauté in the oil until tender. Stir in the spices and cook for
a minute or so.

Add the bean mixture and stir and cook until it is thick but still
moist.

Season with shoyu, salt and pepper.

VEGETABLE FILLING

1 onion
2 carrots
8 oz (225g) mushrooms
12 oz (350g) spinach
1 potato
Half a cauliflower
2 tablespoons vegetable oil
Stock (optional)
1 teaspoon oregano
Sea salt and freshly ground black pepper

Chop the onion, grate the carrots, slice the mushrooms, shred
the spinach and dice the potato and cauliflower small.

Heat the oil and sauté the onion until tender. Add the potato
and cauliflower and sauté for 10 minutes or so. Pour in a little
stock if necessary to prevent sticking. Add the carrot, mushrooms
and oregano and stir and cook a little longer. Season.

When everything is tender, add the spinach and stir until it is
just turning soft and wilting.

81

PASTRY AND PIES

Each morning at the Café, pies, huge, in deep rectangular baking dishes, and quiches, round, risen and golden are taken out of the oven. Despite being an everyday event the appearance of a freshly baked pie always brings great satisfaction.

A slice served hot with a sauce, baked potatoes and steamed vegetables makes a warming meal, and most pies can be eaten cold as well, with salads or just on their own as a snack. In the evening the cooks are usually too exhausted to think of doing any more cooking at home, so they take some of the leftovers with them for their teas, and a piece of pie is often the most appealing and feasible. So it is put into a paper bag and taken home on the bus, wafting tantalizing smells around the other passengers.

Pastry-making

It isn't difficult to make pastry. The important thing to remember is that the butter or margarine shouldn't melt in the making until it reaches the oven. So work with cold hands, cold water, a minimum of handling and a quick, hot oven.

Wholewheat flour makes a light, crumbly pastry that is tastier than white pastry. It is liable to fall apart on its way from the rolling pin to the pie dish, but don't let this worry you because when it is pieced together in the pie dish it bakes perfectly. Alternatively, roll the pastry out onto lightly floured greaseproof paper, turn paper-upwards into the pie dish and peel off the paper. This is a particularly good method for pie tops where a guaranteed, smooth piece of pastry is needed.

All the quantities given in this section suit a 9- to 10-inch (23-25 cm) pie dish.

The air was filled with the warm smell of pastry and simmering spices, and there on the scrubbed trestle table, right in the middle of the bakehouse was the pie itself.
— *The Piemakers*: Helen Cresswell.

SHORTCRUST PASTRY

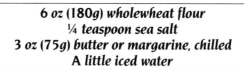

6 oz (180g) wholewheat flour
¼ teaspoon sea salt
3 oz (75g) butter or margarine, chilled
A little iced water

Mix the flour and salt in a large cold bowl. Rub the butter into it, lifting it high with your fingertips until the mixture resembles breadcrumbs. Stir in a little cold water and form it into a stiff ball. If you have time, it's a good idea to leave it to rest in the fridge for an hour or so.

When you are ready to roll the pastry, tip it out onto a lightly-floured board. Always roll in the same direction, turning the pastry rather than the rolling pin. This avoids stretching the pastry, and consequent shrinkage during baking.

Oil a pie dish well and lift the pastry into it. Trim with a sharp knife and prick the bottom with a fork.

Bake at Gas Mark 7 (425°F/220°C) for 15-20 minutes. This is called 'baking blind'.

There should be enough for one 9- to 10-inch (23-25 cm) pie dish — double it, if you are making a covered pie.

Variations:

SESAME PASTRY

2 tablespoons sesame seeds

Stir in with the flour before crumbling in the margarine.

CHEESE PASTRY

2 oz (25g) grated Cheddar cheese

Stir into the crumbled mixture before adding the water.

SWEET PASTRY

1 oz (25g) soft raw cane sugar
1 egg yolk

Stir the sugar into the flour before crumbling in the margarine, and add the egg yolk afterwards.

MUSHROOM AND CASHEW PIE

A pie of creamy mushrooms and roasted cashews, it is a favourite of both customers and cooks. It is quickly made, particularly if there is a prebaked pastry case available. A fifteen-minute 'Mush and Cash dash' has been performed many a busy lunchtime!

2 tablespoons butter or margarine
4 oz (110g) cashews, chopped
8 oz (225g) mushrooms
1 tablespoon wholewheat flour
½ pint (275ml) milk
1 dessertspoon tamari
Freshly grated nutmeg
Sea salt and freshly ground black pepper
1 shortcrust pastry case, baked blind (see page 84)

Preheat the oven to Gas Mark 6 (400°F/200°C).

Melt the butter in a pan and sauté the cashews until just golden. Add the mushrooms, roughly chopped, and sauté a further 5-10 minutes. Whisk the flour into the milk, add to the pan and stir until it thickens. Stir in the tamari and season with a little nutmeg, salt and pepper.

Pour into the prebaked pastry case and bake for 10-15 minutes. Allow to set for a few minutes before cutting and serving.

LEEK AND SOUR CREAM PIE

Double quantity of shortcrust pastry (see page 84)
2 lb (900g) leeks
¼ pint (150ml) sour cream
1 level teaspoon mace
Sea salt
Beaten egg for glazing

Preheat oven to Gas Mark 7 (425°F/220°C).

Line an oiled pie dish with half the pastry and prebake for 10 minutes or so.

Wash the leeks well (see page 24), halve and quarter lengthways and slice into 2-inch (5 cm) lengths. Steam until just tender. Put into a bowl, stir in the sour cream, mace and a sprinkle of salt, and pack into the pie case.

Top with the remaining pastry, trim and seal the edges with a fork. Glaze with the beaten egg and prick 2 or 3 times.

Bake for 30 minutes until golden on top.

FARMHOUSE COURGETTE PIE

Double quantity of shortcrust pastry (see page 84)
1 lb (450g) courgettes
1 dessertspoon butter or margarine
1 dessertspoon wholewheat flour
½ pint (275ml) yogurt
3 oz (75g) grated cheese
1 dessertspoon fresh mint, chopped fine
Juice of ½ lemon
1 teaspoon tamari
Freshly ground black pepper
Beaten egg for glazing

Preheat the oven to Gas Mark 6 (400°F/200°C).

Line an oiled pie dish with half the pastry and bake for 10-15 minutes. Cut the courgettes lengthways into six or eight pieces, then into 2-inch (5 cm) lengths. Melt the butter in a pan and sauté them until tender. Stir the flour into the yogurt and add to the pan. Cook to thicken a little, then turn off the heat.

Stir in the cheese, mint, lemon juice, tamari and black pepper. Pile into the pastry case, cover with the remaining pastry, trim and press around the edge with a fork. Glaze with the beaten egg and cut 2 or 3 small slits into the top.

Bake 30-40 minutes.

COURGETTE AND TOFU PIE

A vegan version can be made by substituting 8 oz (225g) of tofu for the yogurt, flour and cheese.

Simply mash the tofu with the lemon juice, tamari, mint and pepper and stir into the cooked courgettes.

CHESTNUT AND MUSHROOM PIE

9 oz (250g) dried chestnuts
1 tablespoon olive oil
1 large onion, roughly chopped
12 oz (350g) button mushrooms
1 teaspoon marjoram
1 dessertspoon tamari
Freshly ground black pepper
2 teaspoons arrowroot
Double quantity shortcrust pastry (see page 84)
Beaten egg for glazing

Preheat the oven to Gas Mark 7 (425°F/220°C).

Soak the chestnuts in plenty of water for at least an hour, then cook for ¾-1 hour until tender. Drain and reserve the stock.

Heat the olive oil in a large pan and sauté the onion until just turning brown. Halve the mushrooms, keeping any small ones whole and add to the pan with the marjoram. Sauté for 5 minutes, then add the chestnuts, tamari, a little pepper and enough chestnut stock to make a gravy.

Mix the arrowroot in a little cold water, stir into the pan and cook until it thickens.

Bake the pastry case blind for 10 minutes or so, tip the filling into it, top with pastry and seal all round with a fork. Glaze with beaten egg and cut 2 or 3 slits into the top, then bake for 30 minutes until nicely browned.

Serve with a gravy — and perhaps Brussels sprouts and green salad.

RUSSIAN CABBAGE PIE

A delicious yogurt pastry filled with cabbage, sharp apple and soft white cheese.

pastry:

2 eggs
½ pint (275ml) yogurt
Pinch of sea salt
Wholewheat flour, as needed

filling:

¾ medium head white cabbage
2 large cooking apples (e.g. Bramleys)
1 tablespoon vegetable oil
Sea salt and freshly ground black pepper
10 oz (275g) Cheshire or Lancashire cheese
1 egg, beaten
1 oz (25g) margarine
Beaten egg for glazing

Preheat the oven to Gas Mark 7 (425°F/220°C).

To make the pastry, beat the eggs and then beat in the yogurt, salt and enough flour to form an elastic dough. Oil the pie dish, line with half the pastry and bake for 10 minutes.

Chop the cabbage finely, and peel, core and dice the apples. Heat the oil in a saucepan and sauté the cabbage for a few minutes. Add the apples, put the lid on and shake the pan a few times to let the mixture heat through, then steam until the cabbage is tender. Season with salt and pepper.

Grate the cheese and mix with the egg and margarine. Layer half the cabbage mixture into the pastry case, then half the cheese mixture, then the rest of the cabbage mixture, pressing down well, and finally the rest of the cheese mixture. Top with pastry, trim and press down the edges with a fork. Brush with beaten egg and cut 2 to 3 small slits into the top.

Bake for 40 minutes until golden-brown.

Many's the long night I've dreamed of cheese — toasted mostly.
— *Treasure Island*: R. L. Stevenson.

CHEDDAR QUICHE

Once a week, a farmer from just outside Leeds, delivers to the Café several trays of free-range eggs. He is fond of his hens and once gave us a large colour photo of them, pecking about in a field. The eggs have deep, golden yolks and a rich flavour, and so make particularly good quiches.

3 eggs
¼ pint (150ml) single cream
¼ pint (150ml) milk
3 oz (75g) grated Cheddar cheese
A few watercress leaves or fresh chives, chopped fine
½ teaspoon dill leaves
Sea salt and freshly ground black pepper
Sesame seed pastry case, baked blind (see page 84)

Preheat oven to Gas Mark 6 (400F°/200°C).

Beat the eggs, cream and milk together thoroughly. Stir in the grated cheese, watercress or chives, dill and a little salt. Pour into the pastry case and grind some black pepper over.

Bake for 30-40 minutes until golden and risen.

Variations:

Many vegetables can be used in a quiche. Some need to be steamed or sautéed first and others can be sliced straight into the pastry case. For the following suggestions, omit the watercress, chives and dill leaves from the basic recipe, and arrange the prepared vegetables in the pastry case before pouring in the egg, milk and cheese mixture.

TOMATO AND PARSLEY QUICHE

1 onion
1 tablespoon olive oil
1 teaspoon basil
3 tomatoes
1 tablespoon fresh parsley, chopped fine

Slice the onion into rings and sauté in the olive oil with the basil until soft. Tip into the pastry case. Slice the tomatoes thinly and arrange over the onions. Sprinkle with parsley and proceed as in the basic recipe.

BROCCOLI AND WENSLEYDALE QUICHE

¾ lb (350g) broccoli
3 eggs
½ pint (275ml) milk
Sea salt and freshly ground black pepper
3 oz (75g) Wensleydale, grated
Sesame seed pastry case, baked blind (see page 84)

Preheat the oven to Gas Mark 6 (400°F/200°C).

Chop the broccoli florets, stalks and leaves into even-sized pieces, discarding any tough, old stalks and leaves. Steam until tender.

Beat the eggs with the milk and a good pinch of salt and stir in the Wensleydale. Fill the pastry case with the broccoli, pour in the egg-and-cheese mixture and grind a little pepper over it.

Bake 30-40 minutes until golden and risen.

LEEK QUICHE

2 large leeks

Prepare the leeks as described on page 24.

Slice into quarters lengthways, then into 2 inch (5 cm) pieces. Steam until tender, tip into the pastry case and proceed as in the basic recipe.

SPINACH QUICHE

1 lb (450g) spinach
1 tablespoon butter
Grated nutmeg

Shred the spinach and sauté in the butter until just beginning to wilt. Tip into the pastry case, grate over a little nutmeg and proceed as in the basic recipe.

MUSROOM QUICHE

8 oz (225g) button mushrooms
1 tablespoon butter

Slice the mushrooms thinly and sauté in the butter with a little lemon juice, until just tender. Arrange over the pastry case and proceed as in the basic recipe.

CAULIFLOWER QUICHE

1 lb (450g) cauliflower
1 teaspoon marjoram

Chop the cauliflower into small florets and steam until tender. Arrange over the pastry case, sprinkle with the marjoram and proceed as in the basic recipe.

VEGETABLE AND BEAN CRUMBLE

6 oz (175g) red kidney beans, soaked overnight
1 onion
1 large carrot
½ a swede
1 large leek
1 small spring cabbage
1 tablespoon oil
Stock as needed
1 teaspoon marjoram
1 teaspoon thyme
2 tablespoons tamari
Sea salt and freshly ground black pepper

topping:

4 oz (110g) rolled oats
2 oz (50g) wholewheat flour
2 oz (50g) sunflower seeds
¼ teaspoon sea salt
3 oz (75g) margarine

Preheat the oven to Gas Mark 7 (425°F/220°C).

Drain the beans and cook in new water until tender; drain. Dice the onion, carrot and swede small; slice the leek and shred the cabbage. Heat the vegetable oil and sauté the onion until transparent. Add the leek, carrot and swede and sauté a further 5 minutes. Pour in stock until it just reaches the top of the vegetables and then add the beans, herbs and tamari.

Simmer until the vegetables are tender, then add the spring cabbage and cook for a further 5 minutes. Season with salt and pepper. Tip into a well-oiled casserole.

Mix the oats, flour, sunflower seeds and salt in a bowl and rub in the margarine. Scatter over the bean and vegetable mixture and bake for 30-40 minutes.

Serve with a herb sauce or gravy.

TOMATO AND OLIVE PIZZA

sauce:

2 onions
1 garlic clove
1 green pepper
1 tablespoon olive oil
1½ lb (700g) ripe tomatoes
1 teaspoon basil
½ teaspoon marjoram
½ teaspoon oregano
Sea salt and freshly ground black pepper

base:

8 oz (225g) wholewheat flour
Pinch of sea salt
2 teaspoons dried yeast
6 fl oz (175ml) warm water
1 teaspoon honey

topping:

5 oz (150g) grated cheese
1 green pepper
6 black olives

Dice the onions, garlic and pepper and sauté in the olive oil until tender. Roughly chop the tomatoes, add to the pan with the herbs and seasoning and simmer for 30 minutes, adding water as necessary until the topping becomes a fairly thick purée.

Preheat the oven to Gas Mark 7 (425°F/220°C).

Mix the flour, salt and yeast in a large bowl. Pour in the water and honey and mix to a dough. Leave to rise in a warm place for half an hour or until doubled in size.

Knead and divide into 6 balls. Roll each out into a circle and place on a well oiled baking tray. Oil each circle, divide the sauce amongst them and then the grated cheese. Slice 6 circles from the green pepper and place one on each pizza with a black olive in the middle.

Bake for 30 minutes until bubbling and golden.

MUSHROOM PIZZA

Use 8 oz (225g) of sliced mushrooms in the sauce instead of the green pepper.

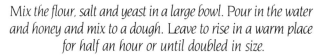

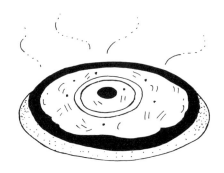

CREAMY CABBAGE AND CORIANDER PIE

Bunches of coriander are cheaply bought from those market stalls which sell the more unusual kinds of vegetables. They are then put into jugs of water to be kept fresh alongside jugs of parsley and mint on a shelf in the Café kitchen. When the coriander is chopped it fills the kitchen with its exotic smell — and its delicate flavour makes this pie of cabbage, carrots and white sauce something really special.

---

3 carrots
½ head celery
½ head savoy cabbage
2-3 tablespoons fresh coriander leaves, shredded
¾ pint (425ml) white sauce (see page 44)
Juice of ½ lemon
Sea salt and freshly ground black pepper
Double quantity of shortcrust pastry (see page 84)
Beaten egg for glazing

Preheat the oven to Gas Mark 6 (400°F/200°C).

Dice the carrot and celery small and shred the cabbage. Steam until tender. Put into a bowl, stir in the coriander, white sauce and lemon juice and season with salt and pepper. Leave to cool.

Line an oiled pie dish with half the pastry and bake for 10-15 minutes. Fill with the cabbage mixture, cover with pastry, trim with a sharp knife and seal around the edge with a fork. Glaze with a beaten egg and cut 2 or 3 small slits into the top.

Bake 30-40 minutes.

ADUKI BEAN AND SPINACH PIE

Aduki beans have an earthy flavour which goes very well with spinach and thyme.

Double quantity of shortcrust pastry (see page 84)
10 oz (275g) aduki beans, soaked overnight
1 onion
1 teaspoon thyme
1 teaspoon bouquet garni
1 tablespoon olive oil
12 oz (350g) spinach
Tamari
Sea salt and freshly ground black pepper
Beaten egg for glazing

Preheat the oven to Gas Mark 6-7 (400°F/200°C-425°F/220°C).

Roll out half the pastry for the base and bake 10-15 minutes.

Meanwhile, drain the beans and cook in new water until tender. Drain.

Dice the onion finely and sauté with the herbs in the olive oil until soft. Wash and shred the spinach, add to the onion and cook until it is just wilting. Stir in the beans, add tamari to taste and season with salt and pepper.

Pile into the pastry case. Cover with the remaining pastry, trim, seal the edges with a fork and cut 2 or 3 slits into the top with a sharp knife. Glaze with beaten egg or oil and bake 30-40 minutes until golden.

Serve with a gravy.

CAKES, BISCUITS AND DESSERTS

She was a person who needed cake.
— *Night and Day*: Virginia Woolf.

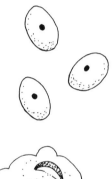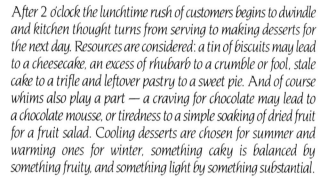

After 2 o'clock the lunchtime rush of customers begins to dwindle and kitchen thought turns from serving to making desserts for the next day. Resources are considered: a tin of biscuits may lead to a cheesecake, an excess of rhubarb to a crumble or fool, stale cake to a trifle and leftover pastry to a sweet pie. And of course whims also play a part — a craving for chocolate may lead to a chocolate mousse, or tiredness to a simple soaking of dried fruit for a fruit salad. Cooling desserts are chosen for summer and warming ones for winter, something caky is balanced by something fruity, and something light by something substantial.

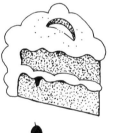

Some desserts are very easily prepared, while others require much care. Cakes are particularly time-consuming for it is most important that they should be well mixed, the margarine and sugar thoroughly creamed and the eggs added very gradually. Some cooks thrive on this sort of work and in the afternoons can often be found sitting on the flour bin, creaming and beating. It is certainly a satisfying job, for the patience of the beating is always evident in the lightness of the cake.

Meanwhile, another cook might be chopping apples or rolling out pastry, another serving a pot of tea or nipping up to the bank; and there is usually some interesting conversation going on. It can be a pleasant time of day when various jobs get done with a welcome calmness after the rush of the morning and lunchtime.

At four o'clock the Café shuts and the cooks sit down for a cup of tea and a piece of gâteau, trifle or fruit tart. Something is needed to help cope with the thought of the piles of washing up waiting in the kitchen. A little self-indulgence is necessary every now and then, and that is why desserts and cakes were invented!

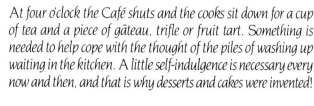

WHARF STREET GÂTEAU

This is a basic cake mix which can be varied by the addition of nuts and spices, and filled and topped with cream and fruit.

---

4 oz (110g) margarine
4 oz (110g) soft raw cane sugar
2 eggs
6 oz (175g) wholewheat flour
1 teaspoon baking powder
A little milk
Apricot jam and whipped cream

Preheat the oven to Gas Mark 4 (350°F/180°C).

Cream the margarine and sugar with a wooden spoon until the mixture is whipped and smooth. Beat the eggs in another bowl and add to the creamed mixture a teaspoon at a time, mixing each addition in well before the next. This takes time and patience but makes all the difference to the lightness of the cake.

Sieve the flour and baking powder onto the mixture, tipping back any bran left in the sieve (the idea being to aerate the flour without losing the bran). Fold in with a metal spoon, treating the mixture very gently so as not to lose any of the air caught by the beating and sifting.

Now fold in a little milk to bring the mixture to dropping consistency and divide between two well-oiled 7-inch (18 cm) round tins.

Bake for ½ hour until the cakes are coming away slightly from the sides of the tin and a skewer poked into the middle comes out clean. Leave in the tins for a few minutes and then turn out to cool on a cake rack.

When ready to serve, sandwich the cakes together with apricot jam and whipped cream and top with whipped cream.

Variations:

SAINT CLEMENTS GÂTEAU

---

1 large orange
1 large lemon
1 mandarin

Stir the finely grated rind of the orange and lemon in with the flour. Stir in the juice of half of each, instead of the milk.

After filling and topping decorate with the mandarin segments.

HAZELNUT AND PEACH GÂTEAU

---

2 oz (50g) hazelnuts
Fresh peach slices

Roast the hazelnuts under the grill, cool, grind and stir in with the flour.

After filling and topping decorate with fresh peach slices.

ALMOND GÂTEAU

---

2 oz (50g) blanched almonds
A few flaked almonds

Chop the almonds well and stir in with the flour. Brown the flaked almonds under the grill for a few minutes and allow to cool.

Sprinkle over the cake after filling and topping.

CAROB GÂTEAU

**2 oz (50g) carob flour
Blackcurrant jam
A few fresh berries such as raspberries, blackberries,
strawberries, etc., when in season; and when not,
grated block carob**

Substitute the carob flour for an equal amount of wholewheat flour. Sift the carob flour in with the rest of the flour. Use blackcurrant jam to sandwich the cake instead of apricot jam.

After filling and topping decorate with fresh berries or grated block carob.

FRUIT GÂTEAU

**A few drops of vanilla essence
A selection of soft fruit — apricots or peaches sliced,
mandarin segments, cherries, halved and stoned,
raspberries or strawberries, halved.**

Stir the vanilla into the cake mix with the milk. Sandwich the cakes with a mixture of fruit and a little whipped cream. Top with more whipped cream and a generous array of extra fruit.

tea and cake and tea and cake and tea and

TRIFLE

A delicious way to use up stale cake.

Stale cake
A selection of fruit — grapes, peaches, apples,
mandarins, apricots, bananas, etc.
Fruit juice
Sherry (optional)
Whipped cream

Quarter-fill a large dessert bowl with crumbled stale cake. Chop the fruit. (If you are using banana or apple chop and soak in lemon juice to avoid discoloration.) Pile on top of the cake and pour on fruit juice and a dash of sherry.

Top with whipped cream and garnish with more fruit such as grape halves, strawberries or peach slices.

ORANGE AND POPPYSEED CAKE

8 oz (225g) margarine
6 oz (175g) soft raw cane sugar
3 eggs
12 oz (350g) wholewheat flour
2 teaspoons baking powder
Juice and rind of 2 oranges
2 oz (50g) poppyseeds

Preheat the oven to Gas Mark 4 (350°F/180°C).

Cream the margarine and sugar until light and whipped with a wooden spoon. Beat the eggs separately and gradually beat into the creamed mixture. Sift the flour and baking powder, tipping back any bran left in the sieve, and fold in with a metal spoon. Stir in the finely grated orange peel, poppyseeds, and orange juice.

Tip into a large, greased and lined loaf tin and bake for 1½ hours until a skewer poked into the middle comes out clean.

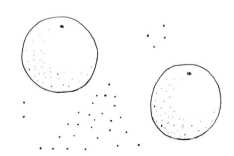

BANANA LOAF CAKE

4 oz (110g) margarine
4 oz (110g) soft raw cane sugar
3 large ripe bananas
2 eggs
8 oz (225g) wholewheat flour
1 heaped teaspoon baking powder

Preheat the oven to Gas Mark 4 (350°F/180°C).

Cream the margarine and sugar until light and whipped with a wooden spoon. Liquidize the bananas with the eggs and gradually beat into the creamed mixture. Sift the flour and baking powder, tipping back any bran left in the sieve, and fold in gently with a metal spoon.

Pour into a large, greased and lined loaf tin and bake for 1¼-1½ hours until a skewer poked into the middle comes out clean.

CARROT CAKE

6 oz (175g) soft brown sugar
6 oz (175g) margarine
3 eggs
10 oz (275g) wholewheat flour
2 teaspoons baking powder
8 oz (225g) carrots
4 oz (110g) walnuts
½ teaspoon ground cinnamon
Rind of 1 orange

Preheat the oven to Gas Mark 4 (350°F/180°C).

Cream the sugar and margarine until light and soft with a wooden spoon. Beat the eggs separately and then gradually beat into the creamed mixture, adding just a little at a time and beating well between each addition. Sift in the flour and baking powder and tip back any bran left in the sieve.

Scrub and grate the carrots, roughly chop the walnuts and fold into the cake mix with the cinnamon and finely grated orange peel.

Tip into an 8-inch (20 cm) cake tin, greased and lined with greaseproof paper, and bake for 1¼-1½ hours. A skewer poked in should come out clean.

Leave in the tin for 5 minutes then turn out onto a cooling rack.

No eggs! No eggs!! Thousand thunders man, what do you mean by no eggs?
— *Saint Joan*: Bernard Shaw.

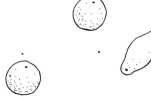

EGGLESS CAROB AND COCONUT CAKE

Carob is rather like chocolate, but with a taste of its own. This recipe uses it with creamed coconut to make a rich, moist, vegan cake.

4 oz (110g) creamed coconut
½ pint (275ml) water
4 oz (110g) carob flour
2 teaspoons baking powder
12 oz (350g) wholewheat flour
8 oz (225g) soft raw cane sugar
Juice and rind of 1 orange
Juice of 1 lemon
6 fl oz (165ml) soya oil

Pre-heat the oven to Gas Mark 4 (350°F/180°C).

Heat the creamed coconut and water in a small pan until the coconut melts, then leave to cool.

Sift the carob, baking powder and flour into a large bowl, tipping in any bran left in the sieve. Stir in the sugar and finely grated orange peel. Beat the orange and lemon juice and soya oil into the coconut and water and pour into the flour mixture. Mix well and pour into a greased and lined 8-inch (20 cm) round cake tin.

Bake for 1½ hours after which a skewer poked in should come out clean. Leave for 5 minutes in the tin, then tip out onto a cooling rack.

HONEY AND CASHEW CAKE

A delicate, light cake of semolina, rosewater, nuts and spices.
Makes 12 pieces.

---

4 eggs
6 oz (175g) cashews
4 oz (110g) soft raw cane sugar
4 oz (110g) semolina
1 tablespoon rosewater
1 tablespoon clear honey
1 teaspoon lemon peel, grated
¼ teaspoon nutmeg
½ teaspoon ground cardamom

Preheat the oven to Gas Mark 4 (350°F/180°C).

Grease a rectangular cake tin 11×7-inches (27×18cm) and line with greaseproof paper; grease again and line with a second sheet.

Separate the eggs and chop the cashews roughly. Beat the yolks with the sugar until light and creamy. Stir in the semolina, cashews, rosewater, honey, peel and spices. Whisk the whites until stiff and fold into the semolina mixture.

Turn into the tin and bake for 35-40 minutes until golden and firm to the touch. You may need to cover the top with greaseproof paper for the last 5 minutes if it begins to brown too quickly.

After baking, leave in the tin until quite cold, then cut into squares and lift each out separately onto a serving plate.

DUNDEE CAKE

A traditional fruit cake. Wrapped in greaseproof paper and foil, it can be kept for up to 2 weeks before cutting. You will need an 8 inch (20 cm) round cake tin, greased, lined with double greaseproof paper, and greased again.

---

3 oz (75g) almonds
5 oz (150g) butter
5 oz (150g) soft raw cane sugar
3 eggs
8 oz (225g) wholewheat flour
1 teaspoon baking powder
Grated rind of 1 orange
8 oz (225g) sultanas
6 oz (175g) currants

Preheat the oven to Gas Mark 3 (325°F/160°C).

Blanch the almonds (i.e., pour boiling water over, leave for a few minutes, then peel). Chop a third of them and split the rest into halves.

Cream the butter and sugar until light. Whisk the eggs separately, then slowly beat into the creamed mixture, adding only a little at a time. Sift the flour and baking powder onto this, tipping in any bran left in the sieve, and fold in. Now stir in the fruit, chopped almonds and orange peel. Tip into the prepared tin and smooth the top with the back of a spoon.

Lay the split almonds in circles over the top. Bake 2 hours. Cool for 15 minutes in the tin, then turn out onto a wire cooling rack. This cake is delicious eaten with chunks of Wensleydale cheese.

APRICOT AND WALNUT UPSIDE-DOWN CAKE

---

2 oz (50g) butter
1 tablespoon honey
8 oz (225g) fresh apricots
1 oz (25g) walnuts
¼ teaspoon cinnamon
4 oz (110g) margarine
4 oz (110g) soft raw cane sugar
2 beaten eggs
8 oz (225g) wholewheat flour
1 teaspoon baking powder
4 tablespoons milk

Preheat the oven to Gas Mark 4 (350°F/180°C).

Grease an 8-inch (20 cm) round tin. Cream the butter and honey and spread around the inside of the tin.

Halve and stone the apricots and roughly chop the walnuts. Sprinkle first cinnamon then walnuts over the bottom of the tin, and then on this arrange the apricots cut-side downwards.

Cream the margarine and sugar and gradually beat in the eggs a little at a time. Sift in the flour and baking powder and tip in any bran left in the sieve. Fold in using a metal spoon. Add milk to bring to dropping consistency and pile over the apricots. Smooth the top evenly then bake for 60-75 minutes.

Leave in the tin for 5 minutes, then turn out upside down onto a serving plate.

This cake can be eaten hot or cold with whipped cream or custard.

APRICOT AND CUSTARD FLAN

flan base:

4 oz (110g) margarine
4 oz (110g) soft raw cane sugar
2 eggs
8 oz (225g) wholewheat flour
1 teaspoon baking powder
A little milk

filling:

2 oz (50g) dried apricots, soaked
½ pint (275ml) milk
3 eggs and 1 extra yolk
1 tablespoon soft raw cane sugar
3 drops vanilla essence

Preheat the oven to Gas Mark 4 (350°F/180°C).

Make the cake mixture as described in the basic recipe (see page 94), tip into a well-oiled 10-inch (25cm) flan tin and bake for 25-30 minutes until golden. Leave to cool in the tin and turn out onto a serving plate.

Cook the apricots gently until tender and drain.

To make the custard, bring the milk to the boil, meanwhile whisking the eggs and yolk with the sugar and vanilla essence until frothy. Beat the boiling milk into the eggs and sugar and pour into a double boiler (if you don't have one use a bowl in a pan of boiling water).

Stir the custard until it thickens but be careful not to go beyond this point as it will curdle. Tip it immediately into a cold bowl to prevent further cooking and pour into the flan case. Slice the apricots in half and arrange over the custard. Leave to set.

When in season try using fresh apricot or peach slices.

BUTTER SHORTBREAD

Makes 24 pieces.

8 oz (220g) wholewheat flour
4 oz (110g) brown rice flour
4 oz (110g) soft raw cane sugar
8 oz (25g) butter

Preheat the oven to Gas Mark 3 (325°F/170°C).

Sieve the flours onto a large board, tipping on any bran left in the sieve. Add the sugar and roughly cut the butter into little lumps over it. Mix and knead everything together until it can be gathered into a stiff ball.

Divide into 4 balls and roll each into a circle about ¼ inch (½ cm) thick. Prick well with a fork and place on a well-oiled tray. Bake in the middle of the oven for 45-55 minutes until light golden and firm.

Cut each round into 6 segments, leave to cool on the baking tray for 5 minutes and transfer to a cooling rack.

Store in an airtight tin.

PRYANICHKI

Makes 12-16.

These are Russian cake-like biscuits, similar to gingerbread in consistency, but with the flavour of lemon and cardamom.

3 egg yolks
3 oz (75g) soft raw cane sugar
3 oz (75g) wholewheat flour
½ teaspoon ground cardamom
Finely grated rind of ½ lemon
A few drops of vanilla essence

Preheat the oven to Gas Mark 7 (425°F/220°C). Grease a baking tray, line with greaseproof paper and grease again.

Beat the yolks and sugar until light. Stir in the flour, cardamom, lemon rind and vanilla essence.

Drop teaspoonfuls of the mixture onto the baking tray and bake 7-10 minutes. Leave to cool for a few minutes on the tray then remove onto a cooling rack.

99

FLAPJACK

Makes 15-20 squares. If desserts for the day are lacking a tray of flapjack is often thrown together before breakfast, because this recipe entails little more than melting margarine and mixing oats and sugar — something that can be done even with half-asleep head and hands.

---
12 oz (350g) porridge oats
4 oz (110g) soft raw cane sugar
1 teaspoon ground ginger
6 oz (175g) margarine

Preheat the oven to Gas Mark 3 (325°F/170°C).

Mix the oats, sugar and ginger in a large bowl. Melt the margarine and mix it into the dry ingredients. Tip into a large, 1-inch (2.5 cm) deep baking tray, press down and smooth out with the back of a metal spoon. Bake for 30-40 minutes.

Cut into squares as soon as it is out of the oven, then leave to cool before removing from the tin.

SEED FLAPJACK

Replace 2 oz (50g) of the oats with 2 tablespoons sesame seeds, 2 tablespoons sunflower seeds, 1 tablespoon poppyseeds.

COCONUT FLAPJACK

Replace 3 oz (75g) of the oats with 3 oz (75g) desiccated coconut.

FRUIT FLAPJACK

Replace 2 oz (50g) of the oats with 2 oz (50g) sultanas or currants. Add ½ teaspoon ground cinnamon.

PEANUT BUTTER COOKIES

Makes 20-22 nutty biscuits that melt in the mouth. Use an unsweetened peanut butter made only from roasted peanuts and salt.

---
4 oz (110g) margarine
4 oz (110g) soft raw cane sugar
3 oz (75g) peanut butter
6 oz (175g) wholewheat flour

Preheat the oven to Gas Mark 6 (400°F/200°C).

Cream the margarine and sugar together and then stir in the peanut butter and wholewheat flour.

Refrigerate for 30 minutes then form into small balls and place well spaced on an oiled tray. Press each down slightly with the back of a fork.

Bake for 15-20 minutes until a deep golden-brown.

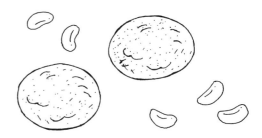

COCONUT BISCUITS

Makes about 20 biscuits.

---
2 oz (50g) margarine or butter
4 oz (110g) light raw cane sugar
1 egg, beaten
6 oz (175g) wholewheat flour
1 teaspoon baking powder
3 oz (75g) desiccated coconut

Preheat the oven to Gas Mark 3 (325°F/170°C).

Cream the margarine or butter and sugar until light and creamy. Gradually stir in the egg a little at a time, beating well between each addition and stir in the flour and baking powder. Put aside 1 oz (25g) of the coconut and stir the rest into the mixture.

Roll into a sausage shape on a floured surface, flatten and cut into ¼-inch (5 mm)-thick finger-shaped biscuits. Press the reserved coconut on top of each and place on a greased, floured baking sheet, leaving room for spreading.

Bake for 30 minutes.

HAZELNUT BISCUITS

Makes 20 biscuits. These are sweet hazelnuts biscuits from Morocco, and very 'more-ish' they are, too! We look a large biscuit-tinful into a Café meeting soon after the first Moroccan Night to ease decision-making, and everyone reached for one 'Khoreybah', as they are called, after another until they had all gone.

---

2 oz (50g) hazelnuts, and 20 extra for garnishing
6 oz (175g) butter
3 oz (75g) light raw cane sugar
6 oz (175g) wholewheat flour

Preheat the oven to Gas Mark 3 (325°F/170°C).

Grind the hazelnuts; cream the butter and sugar until smooth and light, then stir in the flour and hazelnuts to make a dough. Form into walnut-sized balls, flatten and press a hazelnut into each.

Arrange on an oiled baking tray, leaving room for spreading, and bake for 20-30 minutes.

APPLE PIE

The secret of this pie is the cheese pastry. The cheese flavour is subtle and complements the taste of the apple beautifully.

---

3 lb (1350g) Bramley apples
Juice and rind of ½ lemon
3 oz (75g) soft raw cane sugar
4 tablespoons water
Double quantity of cheese pastry (see page 84)
Beaten egg and a little sugar for glazing

Preheat the oven to Gas Mark 6 (400°F/200°C.)

Quarter, core and peel the apples and chop into even-sized cubes. Put into a pan with the lemon juice, finely grated lemon peel, sugar and water and cook over a very low heat for 5 minutes or so. The apple pieces should be tender and falling to pieces a little.

Roll out half the pastry for the base and bake blind for 10-15 minutes.

Fill with the apple mixture and cover with the rolled-out pastry top. Trim, press around the sides with a fork and pierce the top two or three times with a sharp knife. Paint with beaten egg and sprinkle with a little sugar.

Bake for 25 minutes until golden on top. Serve with yogurt or whipped cream.

Vegan:

Use shortcrust pastry instead of cheese pastry and glaze with oil.

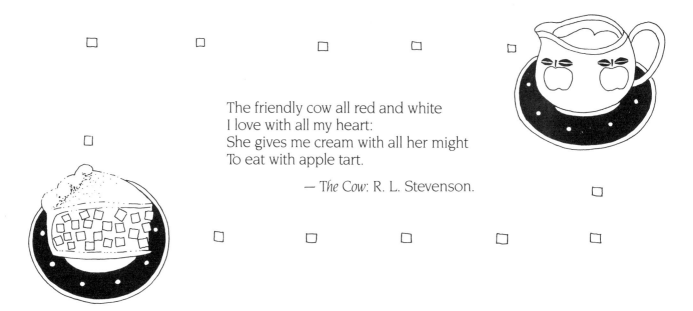

The friendly cow all red and white
I love with all my heart:
She gives me cream with all her might
To eat with apple tart.

— The Cow: R. L. Stevenson.

RHUBARB AND ORANGE CRUMBLE

It has been said that a crumble is everything a dessert should be, soft yet crumbly, fruity yet biscuity, sweet yet tart, comforting and hot with custard or cool with cream . . . And what more could be asked?

base:

---

2 lb (900g) rhubarb
5 oz (150g) soft raw cane sugar (or to taste)
Juice of 1 orange
2 tablespoons water

---

topping:

---

2 oz (50g) porridge oats
4 oz (110g) wholewheat flour
Grated rind of 1 orange
3 oz (75g) soft raw cane sugar
3 oz (75g) margarine or butter

Preheat the oven to Gas Mark 4 (350°F/180°C).

Wash and chop the rhubarb and simmer with the sugar, orange juice and water until tender.

Mix the oats, flour, orange rind and sugar in a large bowl and rub in the margarine.

Pour the rhubarb into an oiled baking dish, top with the crumble and bake for 30-40 minutes.

DATE WHIP PIE

12 oz (350g) dried dates
8 fl oz (225ml) apple juice
¼ teaspoon ground cinnamon
4 egg whites
A sweet pastry case, baked blind (see page 84)

Cook the dates in the apple juice with the cinnamon, stirring constantly until it becomes a thick purée.

Refrigerate. This can be done the night before, as it must have time to be thoroughly chilled.

Preheat the oven to Gas Mark 4 (350°F/180°C).

Whisk the egg whites until peaked and stiff, then fold in the chilled date mixture with a metal spoon.

Pile into the pastry shell and bake for 20 minutes until golden.

BANANA WHIP PIE

4 eggs
4 small, ripe bananas
1 tablespoon honey
1 shortcrust pastry case, baked blind (see page 84)

Preheat the oven to Gas Mark 4 (350°F/180°C).

Separate the eggs and blend the yolks with the bananas and honey in a liquidizer. Whisk the egg whites until stiff and gently fold in the banana mixture.

Pour into the pastry case and bake at Gas Mark 4 for 30-40 minutes until firm and golden.

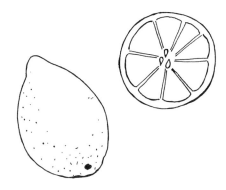

LEMON PIE

Juice and finely grated rind of 2 large lemons
4 oz (110g) soft raw cane sugar
1 oz (25g) butter
2 egg yolks, beaten
½ pint (275ml) water
4 tablespoons cornmeal
1 pastry case, baked blind (see page 84)

Put the lemon juice, lemon rind, sugar, butter, yolks and water into a small pan and bring to the boil, stirring all the while. Mix the cornmeal with a little extra cold water to a smooth paste in a cup. Add to the pan and stir until it is all very thick. Pour into the pastry case and allow to cool.

Variation:

LEMON MERINGUE PIE

Wait until the lemon pie is quite cold. Then, preheat the oven to Gas Mark 2 (300°F/150°C). Whisk the 2 egg whites (left over from the filling's egg yolks) until thick. Add a teaspoon of raw cane sugar and a few drops of white wine vinegar and continue to whisk until stiff and peaked. Pile on top of the lemon filling and spread right to the edges over the whole pie. Put into the oven and turn immediately down to Gas Mark 1 (275°F/140°C). Bake 1½ hours until golden.

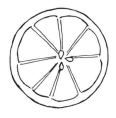

PRUNE TART

Those making Prune Tart at the Café for the first time soon learn that if they want to sample a slice they should put one aside under the counter rather than gamble on a piece being left over. A delicious mixture of prunes and double cream in pastry, it is notorious for being sold very soon after it has been put up on the menu.

---
1 lb (450g) prunes, soaked
1 oz (25g) wholewheat flour
1 oz (25g) soft raw cane sugar
½ teaspoon cinnamon
¾ pint (425ml) double cream
1 sweet pastry case (see page 84)

Preheat the oven to Gas Mark 6 (400°F/200°C).

Cook the prunes until tender. Drain, stone, chop half of them and set the other half aside.

Mix the flour, sugar and cinnamon in a bowl, stir in the cream, then the chopped prunes. Pour into the pie shell.

Halve and stone the remaining prunes, arrange over the pie filling and bake for 30 minutes.

BAKED CUSTARD

---
2 eggs
1 dessertspoon raw cane sugar
A few drops of vanilla essence
½ pint (275ml) milk
Nutmeg

Preheat the oven to Gas Mark 3 (325°F/160°C).

Beat the eggs, sugar and vanilla together in a bowl. Heat the milk until it is just about to boil, then pour into the eggs, stirring well all the time.

Strain the mixture into a greased pie dish and grate a little nutmeg over the top. Place in a pan filled with enough hot water to come halfway up the side of pie dish and bake 40-50 minutes until set.

BERRY CHEESECAKE

For this recipe you will need a 9-10 inch (23-25 cm) ceramic flan dish or a loose-bottomed cake tin, well oiled.

base:

---
8 oz (225g) biscuits, such as shortbread, hazelnut or coconut
4 oz (110g) butter
½ teaspoon cinnamon

---

filling:

---
12 oz (350g) cottage cheese
½ pint (275ml) yogurt
3 eggs
Juice of ½ lemon
4 oz (110g) soft raw cane sugar

---

topping:

---
1 lb (450g) berries, such as blackcurrants, blackberries or raspberries
Raw cane sugar to taste
2 teaspoons arrowroot

Preheat the oven to Gas Mark 2 (300°F/150°C).

Crumble the biscuits, melt the butter and mix together with the cinnamon.

Now grease the flan dish and press the crumbs over the bottom. Liquidize all the filling ingredients and pour over the base. Bake for 75-90 minutes, then put aside to cool.

Stew the berries in a little water until just tender and add sugar to taste. Drain, put the berries in a bowl and return the syrup to the pan and heat.

Blend the arrowroot with a little cold water in a cup and mix with the syrup. Bring to the boil and stir until it thickens. Pour over the berries and leave to cool.

Finally, tip the cheesecake out of the dish and chill until ready to serve.

FRUIT SALAD

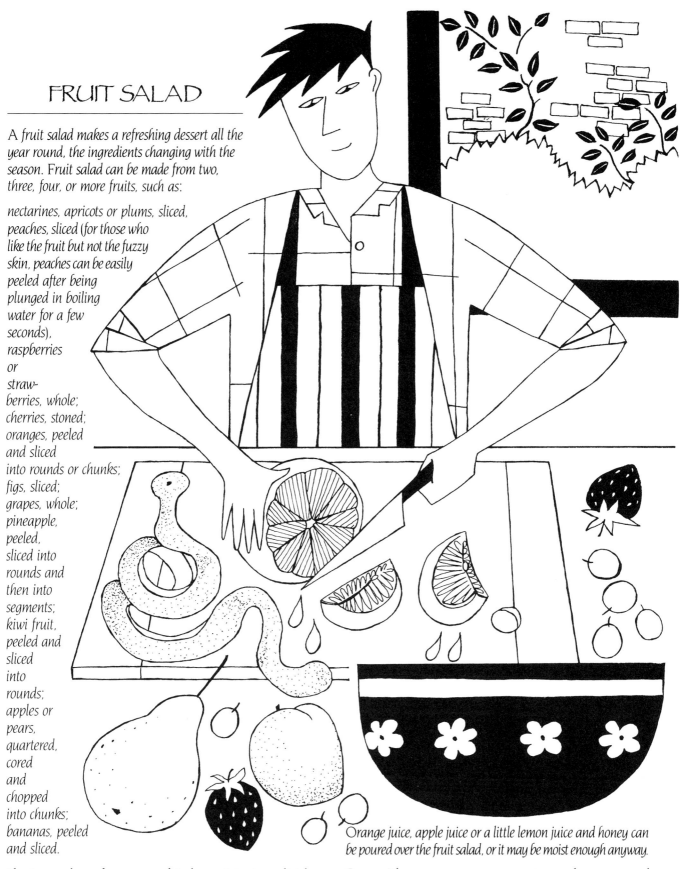

A fruit salad makes a refreshing dessert all the year round, the ingredients changing with the season. Fruit salad can be made from two, three, four, or more fruits, such as:

nectarines, apricots or plums, sliced; peaches, sliced (for those who like the fruit but not the fuzzy skin, peaches can be easily peeled after being plunged in boiling water for a few seconds), raspberries or strawberries, whole; cherries, stoned; oranges, peeled and sliced into rounds or chunks; figs, sliced; grapes, whole; pineapple, peeled, sliced into rounds and then into segments; kiwi fruit, peeled and sliced into rounds; apples or pears, quartered, cored and chopped into chunks; bananas, peeled and sliced.

If using apples or bananas, soak in lemon juice immediately after chopping to prevent discoloration.

Orange juice, apple juice or a little lemon juice and honey can be poured over the fruit salad, or it may be moist enough anyway.

Serve with cream, sour cream, yogurt or cashew cream and garnish with toasted flaked almonds or chopped hazelnuts.

BAKEWELL TART

One of the Café cooks happened to be a proficient jam maker. She made many superb varieties: gooseberry, strawberry, rhubarb, blackcurrant and blackberry throughout the summer and autumn, and in sufficient quantities to last through winter and spring. Breakfasts were marvellous during the time she was at the Café, as was the Bakewell Tart, with its luscious home-made blackcurrant jam base.

Shortcrust pastry (see page 84)
4-5 tablespoons blackcurrant jam
8 oz (225g) margarine
4 oz (110g) soft raw cane sugar
4 beaten eggs
4 oz (110g) wholewheat flour
4 oz (110g) ground almonds
¼ teaspoon almond essence

Preheat the oven to Gas Mark 7 (425°F/220°C).

Grease a 10-inch (25 cm) pie dish, line with pastry and spread generously with blackcurrant jam.

Cream the margarine and sugar thoroughly with a wooden spoon. Beat the eggs separately and add to the creamed mixture a little at a time, beating each addition in thoroughly before adding the next.

Fold in the flour, ground almonds and almond essence with a metal spoon and tip the mixture into the pastry case, spreading it evenly over the jam and right up to the sides of the pastry.

Bake at Gas Mark 7 (425°F/200°C) for 5 minutes, then reduce to Gas Mark 4 (350°F/180°C) for a further 40-45 minutes.

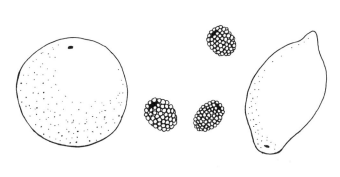

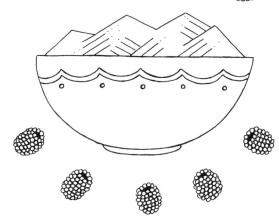

BLACKBERRY SORBET

A delicate fruit ice, deep scarlet in colour and very easy to make. It does, however, require a day when you are mainly at home, for the mixture must be stirred at certain crucial times as it freezes.

---

1 lb (450g) blackberries
½ pint (275ml) water
2 oz (50g) soft raw cane sugar
Juice of 1 orange
Juice of 1 lemon
2 egg whites

Put the blackberries, water and sugar in a pan, bring to the boil and then simmer until soft and fallen. Sieve, stirring through as much of the liquid and pulp as possible, leaving the seeds behind. Add the lemon juice, and orange juice and leave to cool.

Pour into a plastic freezer container and freeze until fairly firm but still liquid in the middle. (This will take about 1½ hours, though it will, of course, depend on the temperature of your freezer.)

Beat smooth with a fork, then freeze again until almost firm. Whisk the egg whites in a large bowl until stiff and peaked.

Beat the blackberry ice smooth with a fork and carefully fold into the egg whites. Then quickly, before the mixture separates, pile back into the freezer container and freeze again. When it is firm, mash gently with a fork.

Freeze until firm enough to scoop out with a spoon and divide into glasses. If it reaches this stage before you are ready for it, leave in the freezer, but move to the fridge 10-15 minutes before serving, to soften.

You may like to serve this with biscuits. The sweet Russian Pryanichki (see page 99) complement this sorbet's tart fruitiness deliciously and will use up the left over egg yolks.

RASPBERRY SORBET

Substitute 1 lb (450g) raspberries for the 1 lb (450g) blackberries.

ORANGE AND PEACH JELLY

The kitchen can become stiflingly hot in the summer when the oven is on, the urn and soup pans are bubbling and the washing-up water is steaming in the sink. An extractor fan hums continuously in the corner and seems utterly ineffectual, though on the occasions when it has broken down the kitchen has, unbelievably, become even hotter and more humid! At such times we fill a large metal bowl with water and ice and take turns bathing our feet, sitting in the yard. Chilled desserts are also very welcome, particularly jellies. Made with agar-agar they are firmer than gelatine jellies, light, fruity and very refreshing.

1 large fresh peach
¼ pint (140ml) water
2 teaspoons agar-agar
¾ pint (425ml) orange juice
Juice of ½ lemon
1 tablespoon honey

Slice the peach thinly. Bring the water to the boil and stir in the agar-agar until it dissolves. Take off the heat and beat in the orange juice, lemon juice and honey.

Scald a serving bowl with boiling water and arrange the peach segments over the bottom. Pour in the jelly and leave to set in the fridge.

BAKED BANANAS

6 firm bananas
Lemon juice
Whipped cream, yogurt or cashew cream for topping
Chopped nuts

Preheat the oven to Gas Mark 5 (375°F/190°C). Wash the bananas and make a slit down the length of each of their skins. Arrange in a baking dish and bake for 30 minutes. Then slice in half lengthways and place in bowls still in the peel.

Spoon any banana syrup left in the baking dish over each, then a squeeze of lemon juice, your choice of topping and sprinkling of chopped nuts.

— o — o — o — o — o —

The constable had to thrust a banana into his mouth to restore his courage.
— The Magic Pudding: Norman Lindsay.

— o — o — o — o — o —

RHUBARB FOOL

2 lb (900g) rhubarb
2 tablespoons water
4 oz (110g) soft raw cane sugar
2 tablespoons yogurt
3 fl oz (75 ml) whipping cream

Chop the rhubarb roughly and stew with the water and sugar until tender. Leave until quite cold, then liquidize with the yogurt.

Whip the cream and fold in the rhubarb and yogurt purée.

Chill.

GOOSEBERRY FOOL

1 lb (450g) gooseberries
2 tablespoons water
3 oz (75g) soft raw cane sugar
2 tablespoons yogurt
3 fl oz (75ml) whipping cream

Top and tail the gooseberries and stew with the water and sugar until soft.

Leave to cool, then liquidize with the yogurt. Whip the cream and fold in the gooseberry and yogurt purée.

Chill.

APRICOT FOOL

6 oz (175g) dried apricots, soaked overnight
¼ pint (150ml) yogurt
3 tablespoons double cream

Cook the apricots in a little water until very soft. Drain, reserving any remaining cooking liquid and chill thoroughly. Blend with the yogurt and cream in a liquidizer, adding a little cooking liquid if necessary to bring to a creamy thick consistency. Chill.

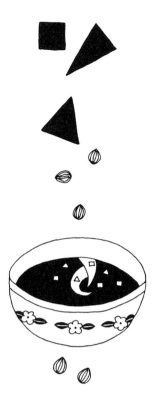

We regularly take our knives to be sharpened at a kitchen shop in the middle of Leeds. The shop sells the most wonderful cooking equipment: pans, sauce and soup ladles, flan dishes and cake tins, ranging in size from the massive to the minute. While waiting for the knives we like to look around, coveting certain choice items, and we usually end up taking something back with us. The manager is charming and friendly and affects a continental manner. He wears a cravat and talks of his latest or forthcoming visit to France to see his suppliers, all of which somehow seems to guarantee the authenticity of his stock.

In addition to kitchen tools he sells a dark, unsweetened and irresistible French chocolate, and this recipe came about to justify buying some!

Frothy, rich and chocolaty, it is justification indeed.

CHOCOLATE AND HAZELNUT MOUSSE

4 eggs
1 oz (25g) hazelnuts
4 oz (110g) dark French chocolate
1 oz (25g) butter

Separate the eggs.

Roast the hazelnuts under the grill, rub off their skins and chop small, or grind.

Melt the chocolate in a double boiler (if you don't have one use a bowl over a pan of simmering water).

Remove from the heat and stir in the butter, egg yolks and nuts. Whisk the egg whites until stiff and peaked, then gently fold into the chocolate using a metal spoon.

Chill.

KOSHAF

We stayed late on the Friday before the first Iranian Night to do some preparation and had almost finished when we realized we'd forgotten to buy any rosewater. Now it is crucial that this dessert soaks for 24 hours, because the rosewater has a very subtle flavour which must be allowed to permeate the fruit and nuts as they swell. It was a problem, and at 9 pm in the middle of dark, closed Leeds, it seemed insoluble until, after a cup of tea, someone remembered that rosewater is sold by many chemists. And so the recipe was saved after a dash across Leeds to an all-night chemist.

This is a very special dessert from Iran, which combines the delicacy of rosewater with the richness of dried fruit and pistachio nuts.

8 oz (225g) mixed dried fruit, such as pears, prunes,
figs, peaches, apple rings, apricots, sultanas
2 oz (50g) pistachio nuts (unshelled)
1 dessertspoon rosewater
½ pint (275ml) water

Wash the fruit and shell the pistachios. Put into a bowl, pour over the rosewater and plain water and leave to soak for 24 hours.

Serve with yogurt. The set sheep's milk yogurt from Greece — if you can get it — goes particularly well with this dessert.

INDEX